Fly-Rod Spinner Baits

Ron Knight

Dedicated to Tom Nixon, one of the all time great fly tyers and innovators.

©2006 Ron Knight

ALL RIGHTS RESERVED. No part of this book may be reproduced in any means without the written consent of the Publisher, except in the case of brief excerpts in critical reviews and articles.

Published in 2006 by
Frank Amato Publications, Inc.
PO Box 82112
Portland, Oregon 97282
(503) 653-8108
www.amatobooks.com

Softbound ISBN: 1-57188-382-7 • Softbound UPC: 0-81127-00216-0

Book Design: Ron Knight

Printed in Singapore

1 3 5 7 9 10 8 6 4 2

Contents

Introduction 1

Tools 3

Materials 5

Wire Harness 11

Spinner Bait - Regular or Round 15

Spinner Bait – Glitter 26

Spinner Bait – Lumaflex 36

Spinner Bait – Other 46

Casting and Fishing 47

Sources 50

Since the day the first cavemen began discussing deep philosophical angling questions, such as the differences in the effectiveness of using a Brachyptera fasciata rather than an Ephemerella hecuba when fishing for early season Neanderthal trout, people have been studying the feeding habits of trout. Detailed and thorough studies have been made of any and every species of aquatic insect, scud, terrestrial insect, baitfish, freshwater shrimp, small mammals and any other crawly-swimmy type of thing that lives anywhere near trout water. If a trout might consider eating one some day, it has been studied. It would take a lifetime to read all the volumes of published materials on the subject. Attempting to read and understand all of this information is even made more exacerbating by the fact that anyone attempting to do so, will usually give up and go fishing long before they complete even the first chapter.

This on-going attempt to understand what trout eat, and the resulting need to imitate it at the fly tying vise, has led to the exponential proliferation of trout flies that so often takes up so much room at the local fly shop.

However, the studies concerning the feeding habits of the various species of warm water fish has not been quite as extensive. I have read several studies concerning the feeding habits of warm water fish, and it appears to me that one of the more prominent food sources for these fish is known by the scientific name *spinner-bait*. Perhaps you have seen these creatures. They are often present in most lakes, streams and impoundments, usually connected to something called a *bait-casting rod*, and in the presence of something called a *bass boat*. Imitating these creatures for proper presentation with a fly rod can often mean the difference between 'a pleasant day on the water' and 'catching a mess of fish'.

An initial observation of these spinner-baits will reveal a relatively heavy lead-head. For fly fishing purposes, this is a strict no-no. Too much weight on the fly can often result in ear piercings in strange and imaginative places such as, but not limited to, your neck, shoulder, float tube, or fishing partner.

Recognizing this major limitation, and tired of being out-fished by those not so inclined to use a fly rod, Tom Nixon set out to find a way to properly match-the-hatch, and create a suitable imitation of the spinner bait for use on the fly rod. His Fly Rod Spinner Bait has saved the day for quite a few fly fishers on more than one occasion.

Using a spinner in conjunction with a fly is not a new or unconventional idea. Many fly fishers, upon first glance, may see the idea as rather heretical. However, adding spinners to a bass fly is nothing new. Cal Johnson discusses the different types of spinners available and their uses in his 1925 book *The Fly-Rod for Bass*. He even advocates using double spinner blades on larger flies. All of the spinner-flies he shows, however, are in-line spinners. Spinner baits have apparently been around as long as bass fishing has, but it was Tom Nixon who first recognized their value to the fly rodder.

It is my intention to write down, here, the instructions for tying and building fly rod spinner baits. Tom Nixon has most all of this information presented in his books *Fly Tying and Fly Fishing for Bass and Panfish*, any of the three editions. Due to the fact that these books are not in print, and are becoming rarer all the time, I want to preserve these instructions before they are lost.

For a disclaimer paragraph, I would like to note that I am aware that as soon as I complete this, I, or someone else, will come up with a different or better way to tie spinner baits, so this should be considered a work-in-progress. Also, I would like to apologize to any left-handed fly tyers that might be reading this. Some of these techniques can be reversed, some won't reverse very well. Either way, I can't tie left handed, so you're on your own.

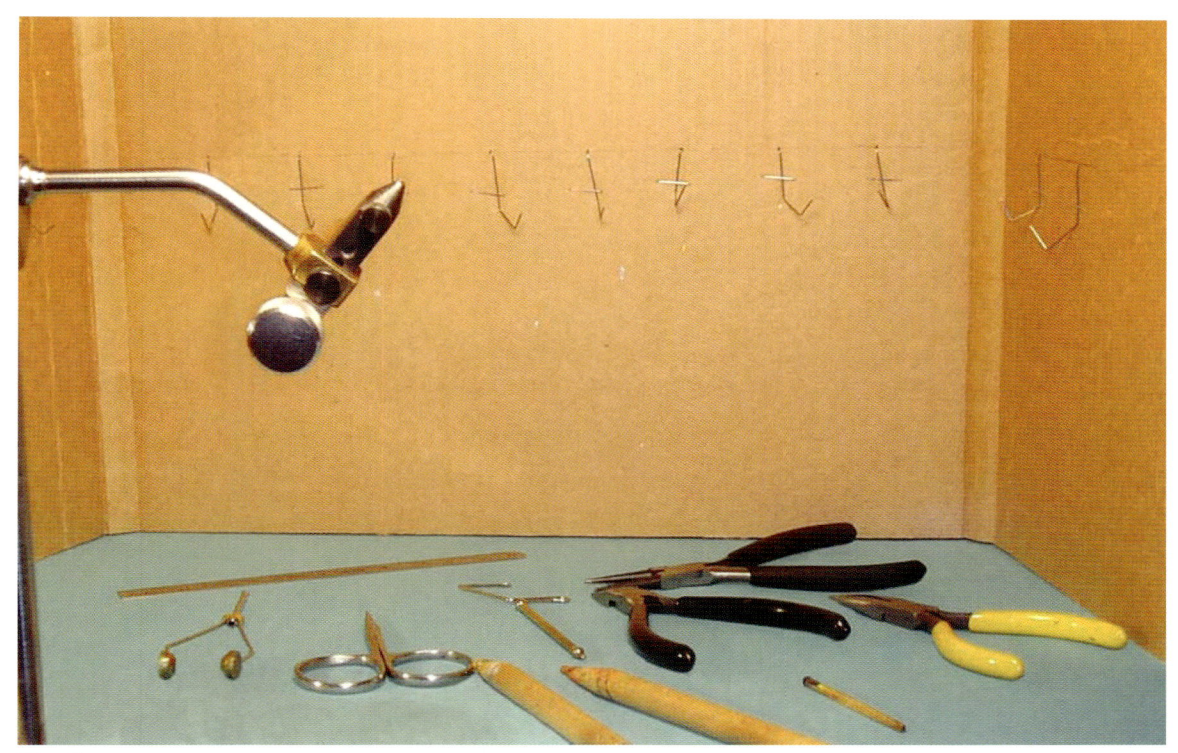

Tools

As with anything else that you may undertake, there are tools that will be needed in order to properly do the job. Many of these tools you will already find on your fly tying desk, so there will be no additional expenditures required. But then, as with anything else we might undertake, we can always find ways to make additional expenditures if we want to, so I'll leave that to your judgment.

Vise – I guess it goes without saying that you will need a vise. If you have made it this far, I will assume you already have one, and will not spend any more time on the subject, except to say that you will need a C-clamp vise, rather than one of the pedestal models.

Bobbin – I like the metal bobbin I have with the flared tip, but bobbin selection is largely up to your individual taste.

Scissors – There are many wonderful scissors on the market today made of the finest quality metal, properly shaped and sharpened for precision detail work. I suggest that you ignore these completely. Working with rubber will dull the most expensive pair of scissors just as fast as it will a cheap pair of scissors that you might find in an inexpensive beginners tying kit. I strongly suggest the latter for tying spinner baits.

Whip finish tool – I like the Renzetti, but you can tie them by hand if you prefer. I would not suggest the Thompson Whip finisher for spinner baits.

Ruler – I use a small metal ruler for measuring the distances on my flies. It is small, about six inches, so it packs well in my kit, and it is not particularly unwieldy at the table. You can pick one up at most any hardware store. I see myself as more of a craftsman than an artist. The artists among you might be able to "eyeball" the amount of skirting material to use, or the length of the tail or skirt. I don't do that very well. Therefore, I measure and count.

Drying Rack – I have a piece of cardboard that I have put a couple dozen wire hangers on. I like to tie several flies at once, so this gives me the ability to hang them all up to dry at once. If you are only tying one or a few at a time, you won't need nearly that many hooks on yours.

Paint Brush – A brush is not necessary if you use a cement that has one built in. Otherwise, you will need a small model builder's brush.

Eye dowels – For painting eyes, I use a piece of dowel. I sharpened the ends so that there are different diameters for use on different size eyes, or on different parts of the eye. You will want a couple of sizes of dowels in order to paint multi-colored eyes. For the smaller sizes, especially for applying the pupils, I often use a match stick that has been sanded down so that it is round on the end.

Wire Cutters – Any good quality wire cutters will work for cutting the wire for the harness. I suggest staying with a quality name-brand tool if you intend to make very many flies. Stainless steel wire is very tough, and will eventually wear out even the best tools.

Needle Nose Pliers – A high quality pair of pliers is up to your discretion here. I use a pair of pliers I bought twenty years ago at an auto parts store—and I'm sure I didn't pay much for them at the time—and they are still working fine. They do need to be fairly small in order to work with small split rings, and to help ensure that the harness loops are small and neat.

Round Jaw Pliers – Here quality is a must. Even the best, highest quality pliers will end up being grooved by the wire. Inexpensive round jawed pliers don't last very long at all.

Split-Ring Tool – I have never found one that I like, so I don't use one. If you find one that works for you, use it!

Materials

Hooks – The best hook I have found for spinner baits is the Mustad 3366. It is a regular length, limerick bend, ring eye hook. It is relatively inexpensive, and is quite strong. While the Mustad 3366 is a good hook, it is not what we would consider one of the more premium quality hooks on the market, Accordingly, the first thing you will want to do, before starting to tie the fly, is to smash down the barb and sharpen the point. I use a small file and hone the point down a little. Proper sharpness would be when the hook point will not slide across your thumbnail, but wants to stick in. I don't usually worry about getting the hook that sharp, since most strikes on spinner baits are pretty serious. However, properly sharpened hooks do help in hooking when the fish takes the fly while it is not being stripped through the water. The degree to which you sharpen your hooks is up to you.

Thread – I like to use size A rod winding thread. This thread is strong and it is inexpensive so you don't mind using a lot of it in building up the head. The strength helps considerably in some of the tying procedures for the rubber skirts. It comes on the usual fifty-yard spools, or you can get it on bulk spools of 950 yards and transfer it to the regular fly tying spools using an electric drill. I took a couple of old wooden spools and used a lathe to reduce the diameter, increasing the capacity considerably so I don't have to load them very often.

Regular Rubber – The original spinner bait used rubber thread for the skirt. Rubber thread comes in several sizes, but the ones commonly used for fly rod spinner baits are the regular and fine (Frog's Hair) sizes. This rubber comes in flat strips that are made up of approximately 46 strands of rubber each. The regular size is approximately one inch wide, making each individual strand approximately .022"

5

square. The fine rubber, also known as Frog's Hair, is approximately 5/8" wide, making each individual strand approximately .014" square. The rubber comes in a larger size, but I have not used it in tying spinner baits. The regular sized rubber is packaged in lengths of 5, 10, 15, 50 feet, or it can be purchased by the pound, which is approximately 83'. The fine, or Frog's Hair, is packaged in similar lengths, or can be purchased by the pound, which is about 166'.

The rubber comes in several colors, but the most popular is black, white, yellow, and chartreuse. Other colors I have used include purple, orange, brown, blue, and several fluorescent colors including orange, pink, and yellow.

This living rubber seems to have dropped in popularity recently, making it difficult to find in some colors and sizes. Several of the suppliers listed on the sources page still carry it, though the colors are becoming limited. I hope this is a temporary set-back, and that production and availability will soon be back up to par.

Round Rubber – The round rubber works in much the same way as the regular rubber. Since the individual strands are round, rather than square like the regular rubber, the individual strands are much more visible in the strip as it comes from the factory. It is available in two sizes—regular and fine. The strip is about one and a quarter inches wide, and is made up of approximately 40 strands, for an approximate diameter for each strand of .031".

The round rubber comes in a much greater variety of colors currently than the regular rubber, though the most commonly used colors are still black, white, and fluorescent yellow. Other colors include brown, purple, blue, chartreuse, red, and fluorescent orange, lime and pink. The fine round rubber is currently available only in white.

Lumaflex – Lumaflex is a very light weight material that can be used for spinner bait skirts. It is basically the same material as spandex. It has a satin sheen to it, and it has a very attractive action in the water. It is packaged and sold in spools. It can be purchased in the 1/4 pound spool, which contains approximately 675 yards—enough to tie several lifetime supplies of spinner baits, or in the large economy sized 2.2 pound spool, or about 5,900 yards for the angler that intends to use a lot of spinner baits over the next three to four centuries. Lumaflex comes in a variety of colors. It comes in the usual black, white and yellow, but there is also royal blue, chartreuse, purple, fuchsia, red, brown, orange and lime available.

Silicone – The last main type of skirting material is the silicone strips. These strips come in a wide variety of colors and styles. It is available in many different patterns of colors, and many have glitter or some other type of flashy material molded into each strand. The multiple colors and styles make the possibilities for spinner bait skirts limited only by your imagination. Silicone skirts are usually available in packages of 5, 25, 50, or 100 pieces.

Chenille – For most of the spinner baits I use, and at least half of them I tie, I use chenille for the body—medium for the smaller sizes, large for the larger ones. Chenille can be purchased on the usual cards, and you can tie quite a few flies out of each one, but if you intend to tie very many spinner baits, it is best to purchase a skein and make your own cards. Unraveling a skein can be a little annoying or messy, but it pays off in the long run. After I have unraveled the skein, I wind it onto large cards that I cut out of cardboard, and I store them in a plastic tub until I need to cut more chenille strips for tying.

Estaz or Cactus Chenille – For some patterns of spinner baits I use Estaz or Cactus chenille. This is a long fibered, synthetic Mylar chenille that adds a lot of flash to the fly. This chenille has longer fibers than the regular Ice chenille, so it gives the fly a little more action, as well as more bulk. It also has the advantage of not absorbing water, so it is a little lighter to cast. I have not found either of these in skeins yet, so if you tie a lot of flies, you will need a lot of packages.

Head Cement – I have used several different types of head cement in finishing spinner baits. Sally Hansen's Hard-As-Nails works well, though I am currently favoring Loon Outdoor's Hard-Head. The Hard-As-Nails provides a good, hard, shiny coat, but it does have the tendency, if you are not careful, to dissolve the acrylic paint used for the eyes. The Hard-Head will not dissolve the eyes (provided you have let them dry properly) but it does seem to dry slowly. Hard-Head also has the advantage of being water based, so it is easy to thin and to clean up.

Paint – I like to use the fluorescent Acrylic paint that is available at most craft or discount stores. The fluorescent colors are much more vivid than regular colors are, and there is a large selection of fluorescent colors to choose from. These acrylic paints are water soluble, so they are easy to thin, and to clean up.

Wire – The best wire for the harness is trolling wire in the .022" size. This wire is stainless steel, so it doesn't rust, and this size seems to be adequately strong enough for the twists to hold. It is small enough to be useful—adding negligible weight, and it is large enough to be easy to work with. I have tries using the same sized piano wire, but I would not recommend it if you intend to tie many flies. Piano wire will definitely wear out your tools—not to mention your fingers—much, much quicker.

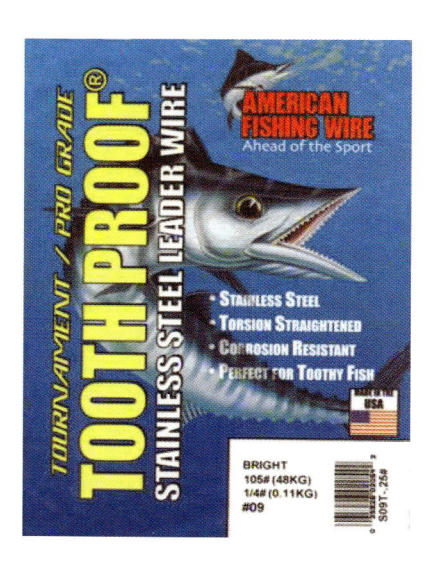

Split Rings – I use size 10 split-rings in both the brass and silver colors. This size seems to work well enough on all sizes of spinner baits that I make, so I stick with just the one size. You can use a smaller size, and it doesn't seem to make any real difference in the performance or weight of the fly, but the smaller size is more difficult to work with.

Barrel Swivels – I use size 10 barrel swivels in both the brass and silver colors. Again, this size seems to work well for all sizes, so I just stick with the one.

Spinner Blades – I usually use the Indiana blades in sizes one through four in both brass and silver. I like the hammered finish, but it is a matter of taste. There are a lot of painted, holographic or otherwise fancy blades you can try. I have not used many of them because I have not yet found any of the real fascinating ones in the smaller sizes that I like. But it is a matter of taste, and I am sure that one day I will find some new bright and flashy blades in the right size, and I won't be able to resist purchasing a bunch of them.

There are many styles of blades available, and all will get the job done. I like the Indiana blade style because it is a

9

compromise in shape. Colorado blades are more rounded in shape, so they spin much easier. This will make them spin at slower speeds, but it can also make them more difficult to pick up out of the water to make a cast. Willow leaf blades are long and thin, and not surprisingly, spin much slower in the water, or require a faster retrieve to get a good spin. Swiss Swing and Reflex blades fall somewhere between the Indiana and the willow leaf shapes. The Reflex blades have an interesting ripple shape to them, just to add a little more variety to your arsenal. I have used the willow leaf and Swiss Swing blades on spinner baits that I intend to use fishing a creek or river where there is some current. When the fly starts swinging across and down stream, the willow leaf blades seem to spin at a more controlled rate than do the Colorado or Indiana blades.

Wire Harness

I will start out by presenting the procedures for building the wire harness, since it is the same regardless of which type of fly you are using.

The first step is to connect the swivel to the spinner blade. As I mentioned earlier, I have never found a pair of split-ring pliers that I like, so I make due with the needle nosed pliers. Start out by holding the pliers in your right hand and grip the split-ring with the pliers, with the split ring opening just to the left of the jaws of the pliers. Because of the way split rings are made, this doesn't work if you are left handed. Next, take the spinner blade in your left hand, and slide it into the opening of the split ring and twist the blade so that it is perpendicular to the split-ring. This will open the ring up slightly, and will leave enough room to slip one end of the barrel swivel into place. Twist the spinner blade and swivel into place together on the ring.

The second step is to begin the wire harness. Cut off a piece of wire approximately five to six inches in length. With the round jawed pliers, grip the wire approximately 1 1/2" to 2" from one end. Wrap the wire around one of the jaws, until a complete loop has been made. At this point, the wire should cross itself at about a forty five to sixty degree angle. At the point where the wire crosses, bend the long end back towards the short end, reducing the angle slightly, to result in a loop which is centered directly below the wire. You may have to bend the short end around a little more to achieve the proper angle for tying off the loop. For properly completing the loop, you will need the wires crossed at an angle between forty five and sixty degrees.

Slip the free end of the barrel swivel over the wire, and down into the loop. Holding your needle nose pliers in your right hand, grip the wire loop so that the loop is flat in the jaws, with the swivel and spinner blade on the right side of the pliers, and the two ends of wire are on the left.

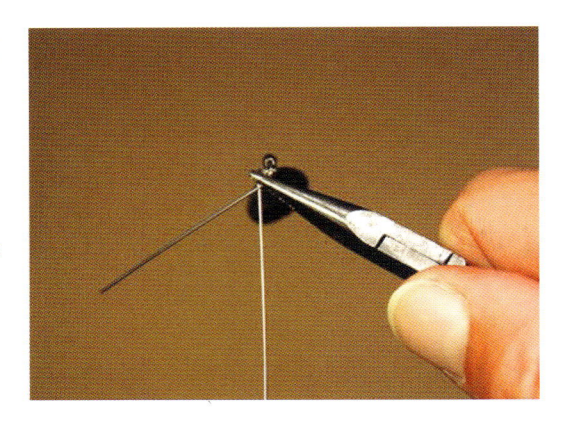

Use your left hand to make two complete wraps with the short end of the wire around the long end. Make each wrap tightly against the jaws of the pliers or against the previous wrap. After you have made the two wraps, the short end of the wire should be pointing up. There should be an inch or a little more of wire left. If there is much less than this, it will be very difficult to remove the excess.

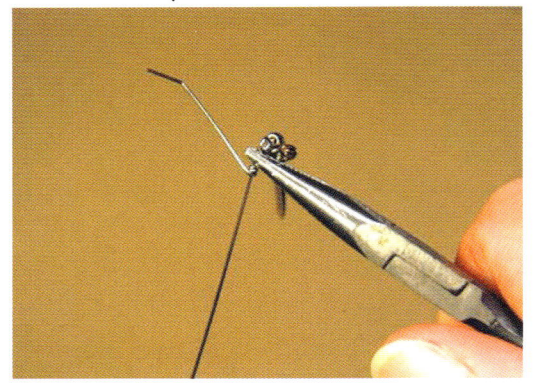

Grip the short end of wire about 1/4" to 3/8" from the end with the needle nose pliers. Bend the remaining end down in the direction of the long end of the wire, to form a ninety degree angle. Grab the loop again with the needle nose pliers in the same position used when closing the loop. Lay the remaining short end down over the jaws of the pliers, so that the recently bent tip is pointing up. Grab the tip, and in a counter-clockwise motion, twist it around like a crank. The wire should break free between one and one and a half twists.

You now have a wire about four inches long with a spinner blade hanging in a loop on the end. You can make any minor adjustments that may be needed in order to center the loop under the wire.

Using the distance referenced in the pattern chart for the size you are tying, grip the wire with the round jawed pliers at the proper distance from the loop to form the eye. Grip the wire so that the pliers are perpendicular to the plane of the loop. Wind the long end of the wire one and a quarter times around the jaw of the pliers to form the eye. Be sure the wire forming the loop lies directly along side each other in order to form a tight loop. When you have finished, both the loop for the spinner blade and the loop for the eye should lie in the same plane. The wire should form a ninety-degree angle, with the eye on the inside of the angle.

Measure the distance needed from the eye to the hook eye loop, and grip it with the round jawed pliers. Grip it, again, with the pliers perpendicular to the plane of the rest of the wire and the two loops. Bend the long end of the wire around the jaw toward the inside of the angle created by the eye. Bend the long end around until it lies parallel to itself. The end of the wire should pass on the spinner blade side of the eye.

With the round jawed pliers in your right hand, slide them up from the bend approximately 1/8" to 1/4" toward the eye, keeping the pliers perpendicular to the wire as before. Bend the end of the wire with the eye, down around the lower jaw of the pliers, to form a forty five degree angle. Move the pliers to the free end of the wire, the same distance from the bend, and bend the free end of the wire up at a forty five degree angle. The two wires should cross at a ninety degree angle, and will form an oblong loop for the fly. Making the loop in an oblong shape helps to keep the fly from fouling around the loop while it is being cast or fished.

It is now time to add the fly. Slip the fly on the free end of the wire. Make sure the wire enters the eye of the hook from the top of the fly in order for the hook to sit properly in the harness. Hold the harness assembly so that the free end of the wire is on top of the other wire where it crosses. With your needle nosed pliers in your right hand, grab the fly loop from the direction of the top of the fly, across both wires. With your left hand, make two complete turns with the wire around itself to tie off the loop. When you are finished, the free end of the wire should be pointing away from the hook and spinner blade.

Grip the free end of the wire about 1/2" to 3/4" from the end and bend it down over the jaws of the pliers to form a ninety degree angle. Grab the fly loop with the needle nosed pliers right next to the wrap, from the direction of the under side of the fly (that is, from the opposite side from when you tied the loop). Lay the standing piece of wire down so that the bent end is pointing upwards, and, in a counter-clockwise direction, twist it around like a crank. It should snap free after one to one and a half turns.

And you are done. Time to go fishing!

Spinner Bait (Regular)

Spinner Bait (Round)

Spinner Bait (Regular or Round)

The original fly rod spinner bait was made using regular or fine (Frog's Hair) rubber thread, depending on size. This rubber is manufactured in strips that are approximately 46 strands wide. The strips appear solid at first, but when stretched and cut, or when they are physically separated, become multi-stranded. When they are separated, each of the strands are square in cross section. The round rubber is similar, but the strands are a little larger, and the strips are only made up of 40 strands each. Which ever style you choose, the tying instructions are the same. Since bulk can become a factor quickly with these flies, I have included a separate pattern chart for the measurements of the regular and the round rubber styles.

Begin these flies by cutting pieces of rubber in the widths and lengths referenced in the pattern chart for the size fly you want to tie. I usually cut a bunch of these all at one time, and store them in plastic zip-lick bags until I need them. It also seems to work best to cut a bunch of strips of chenille, and store them in zip-lock bags until needed.

Place the hook low in the vise, so that the jaws of the vise grip the hook just slightly down the bend of the hook. This will help us later when we are stretching the rubber to make the skirt. If the hook is gripped by the vise too far down the bend of the hook, there is a greater tendency for the hook to slip in the vise, or for the hook to bend when rearward pressure is exerted on the hook as we cut the skirt.

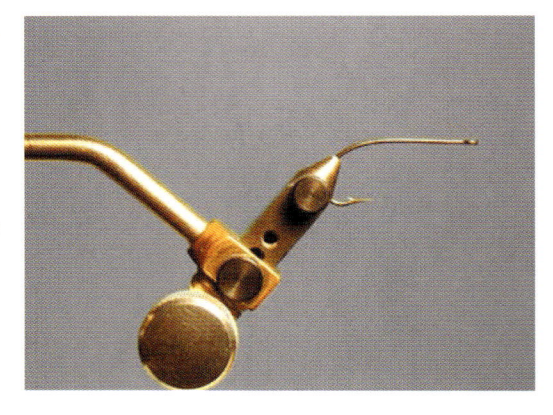

Start the thread on the hook and wind it back so that it is just above the hook point. This is where we will begin tying in the tail. The body will actually start farther back on the hook shank, but we will need room between the tail tie in point and the back of the body.

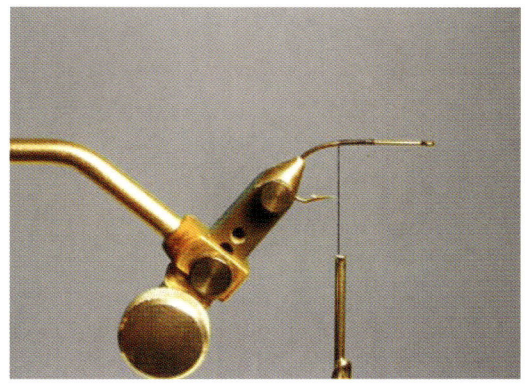

Take the pre-cut strip of rubber for the tail and loop it around the tying thread, and even the ends up. Exact accuracy in evening the ends is not needed—close is good enough. Holding the ends of the rubber tail strip in your left hand, bring the thread up and over the hook shank and secure the rubber tail strip on top of the hook. When bringing the thread on around the hook, make a wide loop forward, rather than coming straight down on the other side of the hook. At the end of this wide wrap, make one more wrap of thread around the hook shank. The thread should now be approximately 1/8" to 1/4" in front of, or toward the eye, from the tail tie in point. Wind the tread tightly back to the tail tie in point. This wide loop forward and the tight wraps back over it will help secure the rubber tail strip to the tie in point.

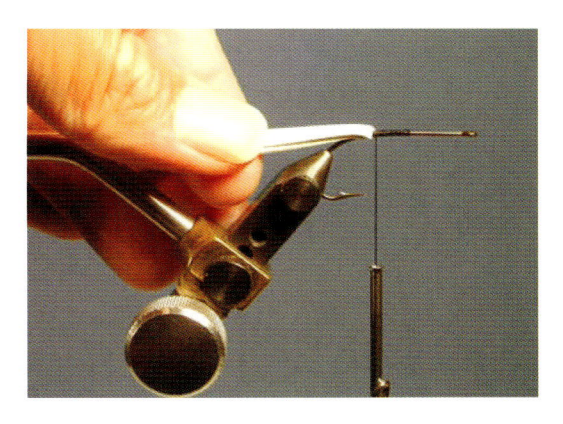

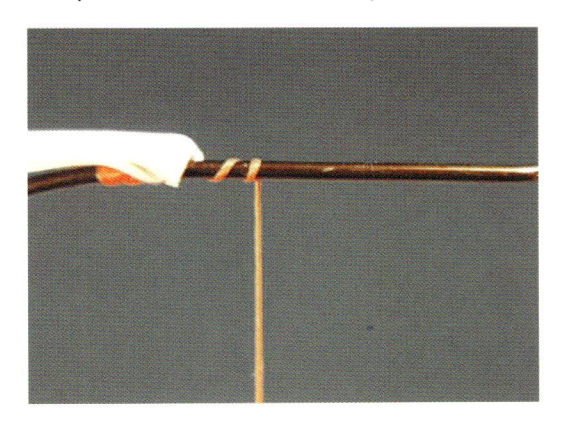

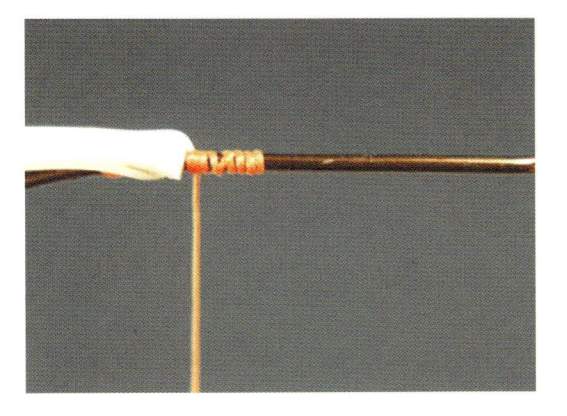

Stretch the tail strip to the rear. You might want to grip the tail strip with your left hand a little closer to the tie in point to prevent having to stretch the entire rubber strip. Stretching the rubber strip reduces its diameter, and reduces the bulk caused by the tail, allowing us to make a smoother body. You can stretch the rubber as far as you like, up to the point where either the rubber or the thread breaks. Usually, if you stretch the rubber too far, (and it takes a good bit of pressure) it will break the thread; in which case you need to re-tie the tail and continue on. We use the size A rod winding thread to give the strength needed to stretch the rubber.

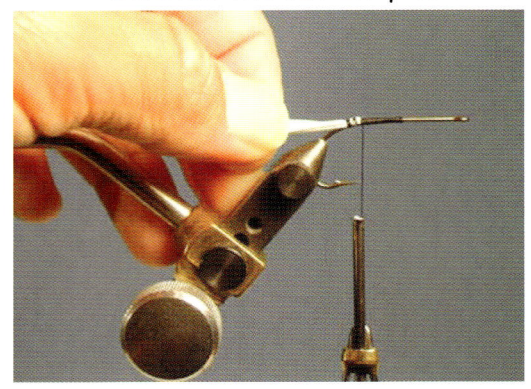

After you have stretched the rubber sufficiently far, wind the thread tightly back over the tail to the end of the hook shank. Make a couple of tight wraps with the tying thread to secure it in that position, wind the thread back to the tie-in point for the tail, and release the pressure on the tail strips.

Wind the thread forward to the tie in point for the body as referenced in the pattern page. This is the distance referenced from the hook eye to the back of the head. It is very important that this distance is left for the head of the fly. This will ensure that the fly appears properly proportional and will also allow us plenty of room for tying in the skirt. The skirt materials can be very bulky, so we need plenty of room to make sure we end up with an even and attractive head.

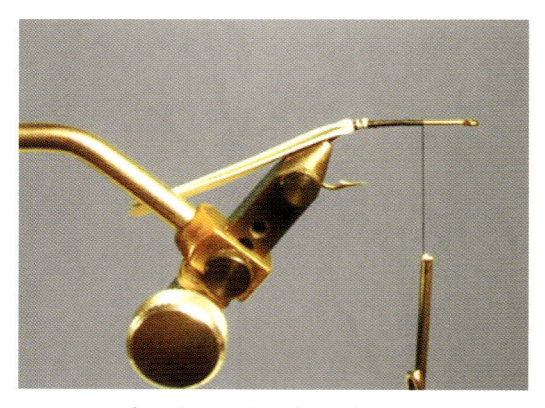

Tie in the strip of pre-measured chenille. Wind the chenille back to the bend of the hook, over the base of the tail, and back again to the tie in point. The object of the pre-measured chenille is to use as much of the chenille as possible. This will help make the body bulky enough to make the skirt stand out well, and to make the fly look like it is a big enough bite to entice a big bass to want to eat it. When you have wound the skirt back up to the chenille tie-in point, tie it down and cut off

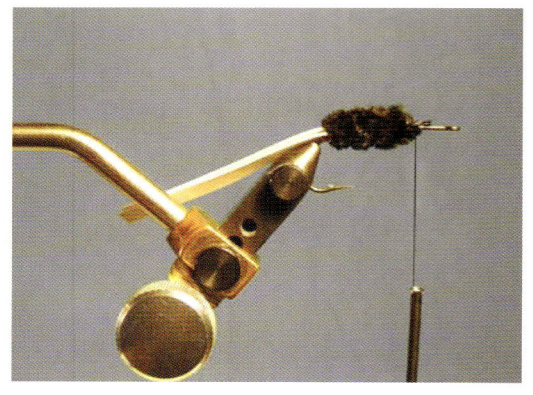

18

any excess.

Wind the thread forward, and stop approximately one hook eye width behind the hook eye. Take one of the pre-cut pieces of rubber thread for the skirt, and cut it in half. Take one of the halves and loop it around the tying thread as we did for tying in the tail, and even up the ends. While holding the rubber strips in your left hand, bring the tying thread up and around the hook shank, and secure the strip on the far side. The wrap that binds the rubber strip to the hook needs to be another wide loop that stops right behind the hook eye. Wind the tying thread, then, tightly back to the tie in point. Again, this wide loop, tied down tightly with the thread will enable us to stretch the thread without any slippage.

Stretch the rubber skirt strips to the rear of the hook as far as possible, keeping them on the far side of the hook, without breaking either the rubber strip or the thread. Wind the tying thread tightly over the rubber strip back the tie in point for the chenille body. Make a few tight wraps, and wind the thread back to approximately one hook eye length behind the hook eye as before. Repeat the process of tying in the other half of the pre-cut rubber skirt strip, tying this one in on the near side of the hook. Make the wide loop forward, the tight wraps back to the tie in point. Stretch the rubber back, keeping it on the near-side of the hook, and wind the thread back to the body of the fly. Make six or eight good tight wraps of thread to secure the rubber in place, and wind the thread back up to the front of the hook.

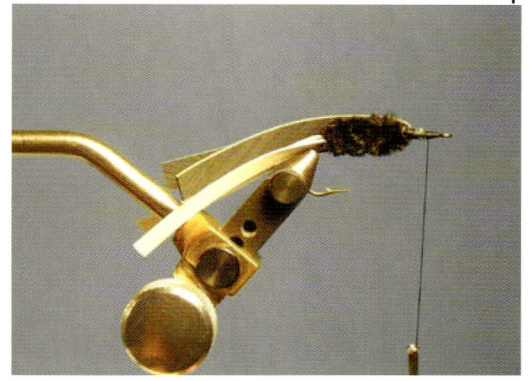

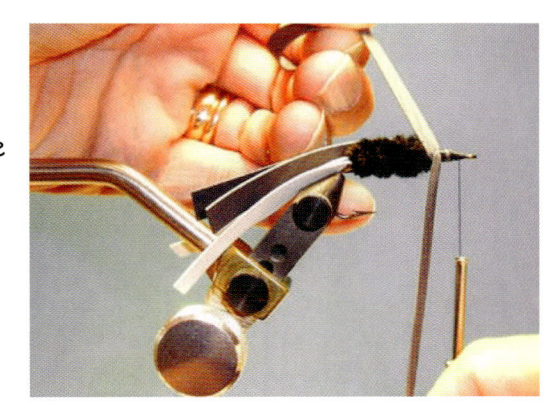

At this point, we need to make sure that the rubber skirt strips are in contact all the way around the hook. Grab one of the strands of the rubber skirt strips on the near-side of the hook with your left hand, and the other on the near side with your right hand, and pull them in opposite directions—one up and one down. As you stretch the rubber and pull it in opposite directions, it will move a little under the wraps of thread, and allow you to adjust it so that it covers the entire half of the near side of the fly.

Apply the same technique to the strands of the rubber skirt on the far side of the hook. At this point, you should be able to look at the fly (rotate the vise so you can look all the way around the fly) and see that the rubber skirt strips completely encircle the hook. There should not be any point on the fly where the chenille body appears to contact the thread head. By doing this, the skirt will appear to wrap around the fly.

Now we will observe one of the other reasons for using the bulky, cheap rod wrapping thread. Return the vise and the fly to the correct tying position, and build up the head into a neat bullet shape, resembling the lead head of the original spinner bait. Keep in mind that the head needs to be large enough to enable us to paint eyes on each side. It is difficult to make the head of the fly completely smooth and even using the rod wrapping thread. The thread is round, and will not flatten out as you are tying. If you are concerned that this will not look smooth and slick enough, you can tie off the rod wrapping thread at any point after the rubber has been tied down, and finish building the head with some flat waxed nylon thread.

I usually just use the rod wrapping thread, and do the best I can in making the head appear smooth. I know I am going to coat the head with at least two coats of cement, plus I am going to paint eyes on it, so a lot of the imperfections left on the head, caused by the round thread, will not be noticeable.

After you have the head wound to the shape you want, whip finish and cut off the thread.

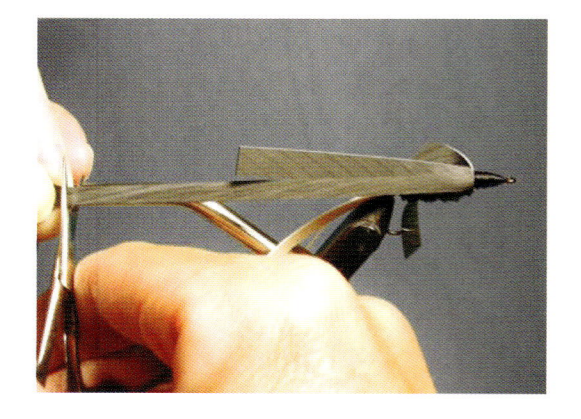

Now it is time to cut the skirt to length and separate the rubber strips into the proper multi-strand finish that we need. Check the dimensions needed for the eye to the end of skirt for the size fly you are tying, and measure that distance from the eye of the hook to the end of one of the rubber skirt strands. Mark that spot with the thumbnail of your left hand, and stretch the strand back several inches. Slowly, cut the rubber strand at your left thumbnail. As you cut through each of the individual strands, they will snap loose from your left hand and hang free. When you are all the way through the strand, all of the strips should hang loose, individually from the fly. Repeat the process with the other three strands of rubber.

Check the dimensions needed for the eye of the hook to the end of the tail for the size of fly you are tying. Measure the distance from the eye of the hook to the end of the tail and mark it with your left thumbnail. Stretch the rubber strand several inches to the rear and slowly cut the strand. As explained above, each strand will snap free from your left hand and hang free as it is cut. Repeat for the other strip of rubber.

If any additional adjustments are needed to make the skirt appear evenly distributed around the hook shank, you can make small adjustments, again, by stretching the rubber strands and gently rocking them back and forth. This will allow them to move slightly, under the thread. This is also the time to make sure that all of the strands of rubber separated when they were cut. If they were cut too quickly, or if they were not stretched adequately, some of the strands may still be fused together. They can usually be easily separated using your fingernails. Often times they will be separated only partially, and will need a little assistance in achieving complete individuality.

It is now time to take the fly out of the vise and put the first coat of head cement on the head. This coat of cement will protect the thread head and ensure it does not unravel. It will also provide a hard and solid base for painting the eyes on. Coat the head with enough cement to cover the threads as thoroughly as possible, without leaving enough to run and drip down onto the skirt. Hang the fly up by the eye until it has thoroughly dried.

After the head cement has dried, it is time to paint the eyes. I find the best way to apply the paint is to shake up the bottle of paint, take off the cap, and use the residual paint in the cap to for dipping your eye dowel. Select an eye dowel with a tip approximately the same size as the diameter of the head of the fly—or perhaps just a little smaller. Dip the dowel in the paint just enough to wet the tip, and touch it to each side of the head. The eye will most likely not appear round since the head of the fly curves away from the flat surface of the dowel. This can be corrected by touching the eye several times in a circular area. The overall appearance will be a circle. I have found that a slight oval shape to the eye looks even better than a small round eye. A prominent eye vastly adds to the overall appearance of the fly. After the first color is applied, hang the fly up once again, and allow it to dry.

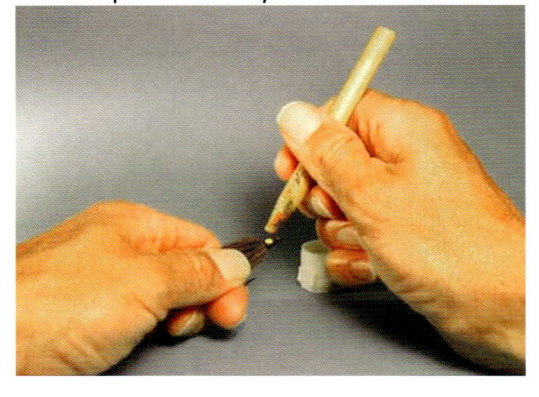

Next, select a smaller dowel, and the next color for the eye, and repeat the painting process. I usually paint the eye with each additional color moved to the front of the previous one, to give the overall appearance of the fly "looking" forward. An interesting effect can also be attained by placing each subsequent layer toward the back of the previous layer, giving the effect that the fly is "looking" back at something that might be chasing it. I haven't heard any complaints from the fish on either style. When you are done, return the fly to the drying rack.

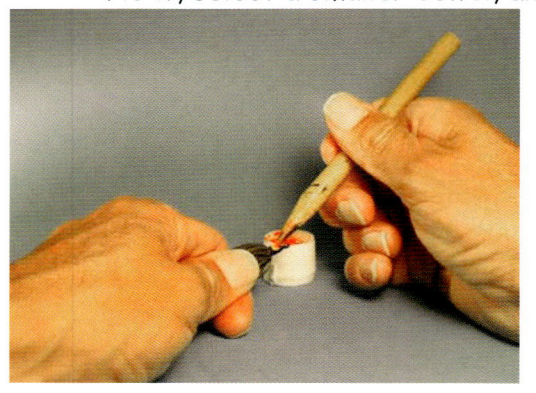

The last step in painting the eye is to paint a small black pupil. Again, this can be centered, in the front, back, or anywhere you like the effect. And again, hang the fly up to dry.

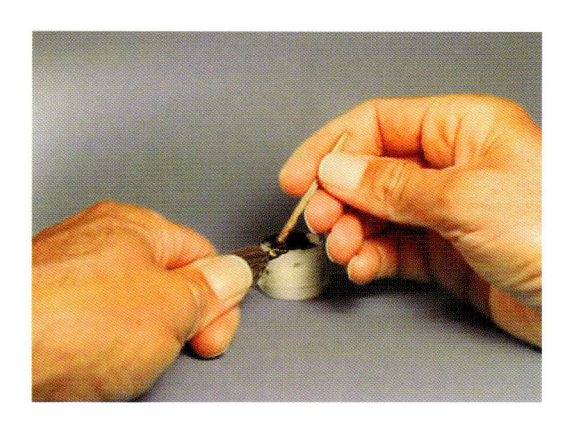

After the eyes have dried thoroughly, it is time for another coat of head cement. This coat will give the head a finished, glossy look, and will protect the eye and the threads. In the event that you choose to use Hard-As-Nails for the cement, care must be taken to keep the cement from dissolving the eyes and causing them to smear out. In this case, allow plenty of time for the eyes to completely dry—a couple of days if you can. When you put the cement over the eyes, make no more brush strokes than are absolutely necessary. Usually, you have time for one or two quick strokes over the eye before the paint softens enough to be affected by the brush. A third or fourth brush stroke may be one too many. Water based cements do not have this problem, and you will have more time to apply the coat. Put the cement on evenly, and, once again, return the fly to its place on the drying rack.

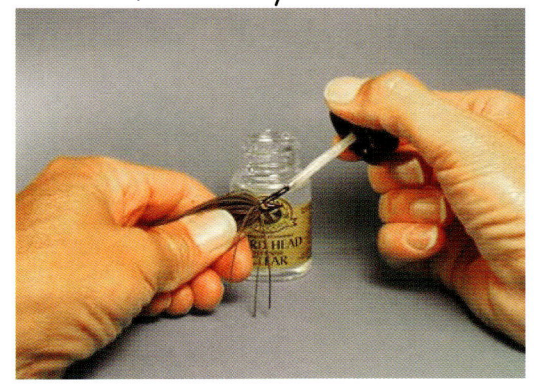

When the fly is dry, it is time to build the wire harness.

Spinner Bait (Regular)

Hook: Mustad 3366 sizes 2/0 - 4
Thread: Size A rod wrapping thread
Tail: Rubber thread
Body: Chenille (2 layers)
Skirt: Rubber thread
Head: Thread built up in a bullet shape, one coat of cement under, and one coat over the eyes
Eyes: Acrylic paint; black over fluorescent orange over fluorescent yellow on black thread; black over fluorescent yellow over fluorescent red on white thread
Wire: .022" trolling wire
Swivel: Size 10 barrel swivel
Split Rings: Size 10
Spinner: Indiana

Colors -	Tail	Body	Skirt	Thread
Black	White	Black	Black	Black
Yellow	Yellow	Fl. Orange	Yellow	Black
Chartreuse	Chartreuse	White	Chartreuse	Black
White	White	Fl. Yellow	White	White
Purple	Purple	Purple	Purple	Black

Fly Dimensions -	Size 2/0	Size 1/0	Size 1	Size 2	Size 4
Eye to back of head	3/8"	3/8"	5/16"	5/16"	1/4"
Eye to end of skirt	2 1/4"	2 1/8"	2"	1 3/4"	1 1/2"
Eye to end of tail	3"	2 7/8"	2 3/4"	2 1/4"	1 7/8"

Harness Dimensions -	Size 2/0	Size 1/0	Size 1	Size 2	Size 4
Eye to hook*	1 1/8"	1 1/16"	1"	1"	15/16"
Eye to swivel	9/16"	1/2"	1/2"	1/2"	7/16"

*The loop for the hook eye should be approximately 1/4" long. The 1/4" loop in included in the measurements above

Preparation Sizes -	Tail	Body	Skirt
Size 2/0	Regular 10 x 5"	Large 11"	Regular 14 x 11"
Size 1/0	Regular 9 x 5"	Large 10"	Regular 13 x 10"
Size 1	Regular 8 x 4"	Large 9"	Regular 12 x 9"
Size 2	Fine 10 x 4"	Medium 8"	Fine 15 x 9"
Size 4	Fine 8 x 4"	Medium 7"	Fine 13 x 8"

Blade Sizes -
Size 2/0 #4
Size 1/0 #3
Size 1 #2
Size 2 #2
Size 4 #1

Spinner Bait (Round)

Hook:	Mustad 3366 sizes 2/0 - 4
Thread:	Size A rod wrapping thread
Tail:	Round rubber thread
Body:	Chenille (2 layers)
Skirt:	Round rubber thread
Head:	Thread built up in a bullet shape, one coat of cement under, and one coat over the eyes
Eyes:	Acrylic paint; black over fluorescent orange over fluorescent yellow on black thread; black over fluorescent yellow over fluorescent red on white thread
Wire:	.022" trolling wire
Swivel:	Size 10 barrel swivel
Split Rings:	Size 10
Spinner:	Indiana

Colors -

	Tail	Body	Skirt	Thread
Black	White	Black	Black	Black
Yellow	Yellow	Fl. Orange	Yellow	Black
Lime	Lime	Fl. Green	Lime	Black
White	White	Fl. Yellow	White	White
Red	Red	Red	Red	White

Fly Dimensions -

	Size 2/0	Size 1/0	Size 1	Size 2	Size 4
Eye to back of head	3/8"	3/8"	5/16"	5/16"	1/4"
Eye to end of skirt	2 1/4"	2 1/8"	2"	1 3/4"	1 1/2"
Eye to end of tail	3"	2 7/8"	2 3/4"	2 1/4"	1 7/8"

Harness Dimensions -

	Size 2/0	Size 1/0	Size 1	Size 2	Size 4
Eye to hook*	1 1/8"	1 1/16"	1"	1"	15/16"
Eye to swivel	9/16"	1/2"	1/2"	1/2"	7/16"

*The loop for the hook eye should be approximately 1/4" long. The 1/4" loop in included in the measurements above

Preparation Sizes -

	Tail	Body	Skirt
Size 2/0	8 x 5"	Large 11"	11 x 11"
Size 1/0	7 X 5"	Large 10"	10 X 10"
Size 1	6 x 4"	Large 9"	10 x 9"
Size 2	5 X 4"	Medium 8"	9 X 9"
Size 4	4 x 3"	Medium 7"	8 x 8"

Blade Sizes -

Size 2/0	#4
Size 1/0	#3
Size 1	#2
Size 2	#2
Size 4	#1

Spinner Bait (Glitter)

The development of silicone skirting material has made the possibilities for color combinations in spinner baits nearly limitless. Silicone can be manufactured in any number of colors, with the possibility of glitter embedded in the strands, or multiple kinds of patterns in the colors on each strand.

Silicon skirting material comes in small strips approximately six inches in length. About 1/4" to 1/2" on each end of each strip of the silicon strip is solid, and the strip is cut into approximately 20 individual strands in between. Since the material is different than the regular or round rubber, the tying instructions are a little different.

Place the hook low in the vise, so that the jaws of the vise grip the hook just slightly down the bend of the hook. This will help us later when we are stretching the skirting material during the tying process. If the hook is gripped by the vise too far down the bend of the hook, there is a greater tendency for the hook to slip in the vise, or for the hook to bend when rearward pressure is exerted on the hook as we adjust the skirt. The silicone will not be stretched as much as the rubber is, so the positioning is not as critical, but the hook is still liable to slip if it is not securely gripped by the vise.

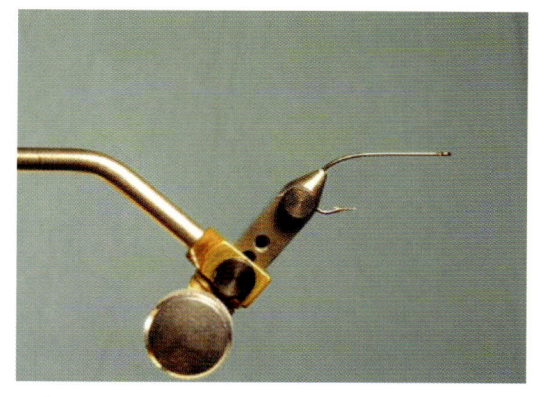

Start the thread on the hook and wind it back to just above the hook point. This is where we will begin tying in the tail. The body will actually start farther back on the hook shank, but we will need room between the tail tie-in point and the back of the body.

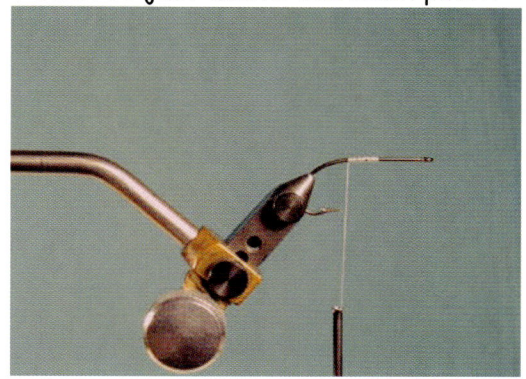

To cut the silicone strips into the smaller fractional pieces that are needed, fold one end of the strip in half lengthwise, and cut it. After cutting, or tearing the other end at the same place, you will have the two halves. Repeat the procedure on the halves to get quarters.

Loop the appropriate piece of silicone strip around the thread. Holding the ends of the silicone tail strip in your left hand, bring the thread up and over the hook shank and secure the strip to the top of the hook. When bringing the thread on around the hook, make a wide loop forward, rather than straight down on the other side of the hook. At the end of this wide forward wrap, make one more wrap of thread around the hook shank. The thread should now be approximately 1/8" to 1/4" in front, or toward the eye, from the tail tie-in point. Wind the thread tightly back to the tail tie-in point. This wide loop forward and the tight wraps back over it will help secure the rubber tail strip to the tie-in point.

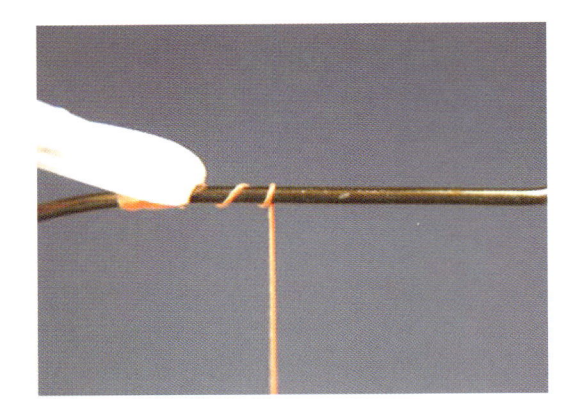

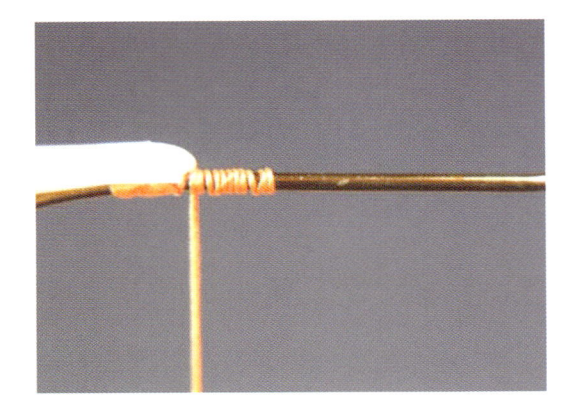

Stretch the tail strip to the rear. Silicone is more fragile than rubber, so use caution not to stretch too far. Stretching the silicone strip reduces its diameter, and reduces the bulk caused by the tail, allowing us to make a smoother body. Because the silicone is relatively fragile, there will be more bulk left under the thread on this fly, but with practice you should be able to keep it to a minimum.

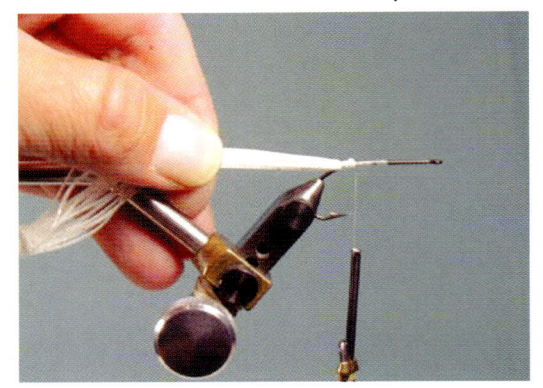

After you have stretched the tail sufficiently far, wind the thread fairly tightly back over the tail to the end of the hook shank. The size A rod winding thread is much tougher than the silicone, so it is very easy to cut through the silicone. It may take some practice, and a few wasted pieces of silicone to judge just how much pressure can be used. Make a couple of secure wraps with the tying thread to hold it in that position, wind the thread back to the tie in point, and release the pressure on the tail strips.

Silicone is not only bulkier than rubber skirts, it is also heavier. Accordingly, I like to use a chenille for the body that will not absorb much water. Estaz or Cactus chenille is made of Mylar, so it is lighter than regular chenille, and will not absorb water. We can also get a lot of interesting colors, including opalescent and dyed opalescent colors in these materials, so we can achieve some interesting contrasts or color combinations to go with the silicone skirts.

Tie the Estaz in at the tail and wind the thread forward to the correct point, indicated on the pattern chart, for the back of the head. Special care needs to be taken not to crowd the head on this fly. As stated previously, silicone will result in more bulk, so crowding the head any at all will result in an unsightly head, not to mention a lot of anguish in completing the fly.

While winding the Estaz forward, keep pulling the fibers back out of the way with your left hand, so that none of the fibers are tied down by successive wraps. The long fibers on the Estaz will help with the appearance of bulk in the fly. When you get to the front of the body, tie and cut off the Estaz.

Wind the thread forward, and stop approximately one hook-eye width behind the hook-eye. In tying in the skirt, cut each full piece of silicone in half, lengthwise. The largest size piece of silicone that can be successfully tied on at once is 1/2 piece. For tying a size 1 fly, you should have two halves, and another quarter piece ready to tie in. Take one of the halves and loop it around the tying thread as we did for tying in the tail, and even up the ends. While holding the ends in your left hand, bring the tying thread up and around the hook shank, and secure it on the far side. When tying a fly that requires three individual pieces of silicone, you will need to tie the first piece low on the far side of the hook. The three pieces will ultimately need to be distributed evenly around the hook. The thread wrap that binds the silicone strip to the hook needs to be another wide loop forward that stops right behind the hook eye. Wind the tying thread tightly back to the tie-in point. Again, this wide loop, tied down tightly with the thread will enable us to stretch the silicone without any slippage.

Stretch the silicone strip to the rear of the hook as far as possible without breaking any of the strands. Again, keep in mind that silicone is relatively fragile, and will break if too much pressure is applied. It is common, during the tying process, to loose a few strands of the skirt. The fish have not yet been observed to count the remaining strands, so the loss of a few is not cause for any undue angst. Wind the tying thread fairly tightly over the silicone strip back the tie in point for the body. Make a few secure wraps, and wind the thread back to approximately one hook-eye length behind the hook-eye as before. Repeat the process of tying in the other half of the silicone strip, tying this one in on the near side of the hook. Again, if there are to be three pieces of silicone to the skirt, keep the second tie fairly low on the near side of the hook shank. Make the wide loop forward, and the tight wraps back to the tie-in point. Stretch the silicone strip back and wind the thread back to the body of the fly. On flies that require three pieces for the skirt, repeat the process, tying the third (the smallest of the three) on top of the hook shank.

At this point, we need to make sure that the silicone skirt appears uniform all the way around the hook. Grab some of the strands of the skirt on the top of the fly, and gently stretch them upward, making a gentle back and forth rocking motion to help even up the skirt. Do the same thing on the bottom of the fly. Rotate the fly to see that the skirt appears to completely encircle the fly.

Now it is time to cover up the butt ends of the skirt with the thread and build it up into a neat bullet shape. Keep in mind that the head needs to be large enough to enable us to paint eyes on each side, though, with the additional bulk of the silicone, this usually isn't a problem. It is difficult to make the head of the fly completely smooth and even using the rod wrapping thread. The thread is round, and will not flatten out as you are tying. If you are concerned that this will not look smooth and slick enough, you can tie off the rod wrapping thread at any point after the rubber has been tied down, and finish building the head with some flat waxed nylon thread.

I usually just use the rod wrapping thread, and do the best I can in making the head appear smooth. I know I am going to coat the head with at least two coats of cement, plus I am going to paint eyes on it, so a lot of the imperfections left on the head, caused by the round thread, will not be noticeable. The important thing is to try and eliminate as many bumps and bulges, caused by the butt ends of the silicone, as possible.

After you have the head wound to the shape you want, whip finish and cut off the thread.

At this point it is time to cut the skirt to length. Check the dimensions needed for the eye to the end of skirt for the size fly you are tying, and measure that distance from the eye of the hook to the end of one of the silicone skirt strands on top of the hook. Hold on to the portion of the skirt that covers the top of the fly with your left hand and, without stretching the skirt any, measure the proper length and make the cut. Now that the skirt on the top of the fly is the correct length, fold all of the skirt forward and, using the strands that you just cut for a guide, cut the rest of the strands off evenly.

Check the dimensions needed for the eye of the hook to the end of the tail for the size of fly you are tying. Hold the silicone strands of the tail with your left hand and, without stretching them, measure the correct distance and cut the tail to length.

If any additional adjustments are needed to make the skirt appear evenly distributed around the hook shank, you can make small adjustments, again, by carefully stretching the skirt strands and gently rocking them back and forth.

It is now time to take the fly out of the vise and put the first coat of head cement on the head. This coat of cement will protect the thread head and ensure it does not unravel. It will also provide a hard and solid base for painting the eyes on. Coat the head with enough cement to cover the threads as thoroughly as possible, without leaving enough to run and drip down onto the skirt. Hang the fly up by the eye until it has thoroughly dried.

After the head cement has dried, it is time to paint the eyes. I find the best way to apply the paint is to shake up the bottle of paint, take off the cap, and use the residual paint in the cap for dipping your eye dowel. Select an eye dowel with a tip approximately the same size as the diameter of the head of the fly—or perhaps just a little smaller. Dip the dowel in the paint just enough to wet the tip, and touch it to each side of the head. The eye will most likely not appear round since the head of the fly curves away from the flat surface of the dowel. This can be corrected by touching the eye several times in a circular area. The overall appearance will be a circle. I have found that a slight oval shape to the eye looks even better than a small round eye. A prominent eye vastly adds to the overall appearance of the fly. After the first color is applied, hang the fly up once again, and allow it to dry.

Next, select a smaller dowel, and the next color for the eye, and repeat the painting process. I usually paint the eye with each additional color moved to the front of the previous one, to give the overall appearance of the fly "looking" forward. An interesting effect can also be attained by placing each subsequent layer toward the back of the previous layer, giving the effect that the fly is "looking" back at something that might be chasing it. Whichever style you decide to use, the fish don't seem to have a real preference. When you are done, return the fly to the drying rack.

The last step in painting the eye is to paint a small black pupil. Again, this can be centered, in the front, back, or anywhere you like the effect. And again, hang the fly up to dry.

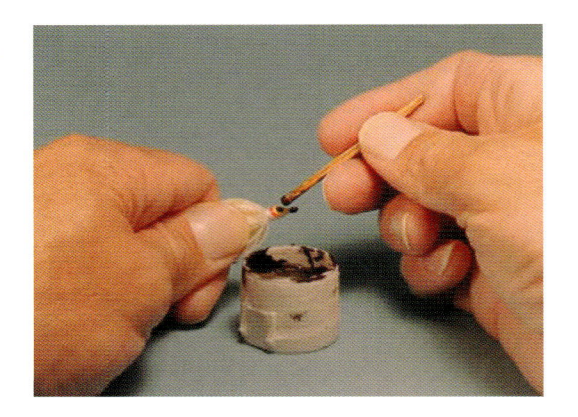

After the eyes have dried thoroughly, it is time for another coat of head cement. This coat will give the head a finished, glossy look, and will protect the eye and the threads. In the event that you choose to use Hard-As-Nails for the cement, care must be taken to keep the cement from dissolving the eyes and causing them to smear out. In this case, allow plenty of time for the eyes to completely dry—a couple of days if you can. When you put the cement over the eyes, make no more brush strokes than are absolutely necessary. Usually, you have time for one or two quick strokes over the eye before the paint softens enough to be affected by the brush. A third or fourth brush stroke may be one too many. Water based cements do not have this problem, and you will have more time to apply the coat. Put the cement on evenly, and, once again, return the fly to its place on the drying rack.

When the fly is dry, it is time to build the wire harness.

Spinner Bait (Glitter)

Hook:	Mustad 3366 sizes 2/0 - 4
Thread:	Size A rod wrapping thread
Tail:	Sparkle Flake Sili Legs
Body:	Estaz
Skirt:	Sparkle Flake Sili Legs
Head:	Thread built up in a bullet shape, one coat of cement under, and one coat over the eyes
Eyes:	Acrylic paint; black over fluorescent orange over fluorescent yellow on black thread; black over fluorescent yellow over fluorescent red on white thread
Wire:	.022" trolling wire
Swivel:	Size 10 barrel swivel
Split Rings:	Size 10
Spinner:	Indiana

Colors -

	Tail	Body	Skirt	Thread
Black	Black/Gold	Black (#21)	Black/Gold	Black
White	White/Silver	Fl. Yellow (#24)	White/Silver	White
Chartreuse	Chartreuse/Silver	Pearl (#02)	Chartreuse/Silver	White
Purple	Purple/Blue	Royal Blue (#04)	Purple/Blue	Black
Blue	Blue/Silver	Silver tinsel chenille	Blue/Silver	Black

Skirt and Tail -

	Tail	Skirt
Size 2/0	20 strands (1/2 pc)	60 strands (1 1/2 pc)
Size 1/0	20 strands (1/2 pc)	50 strands (1 1/4 pc)
Size 1	20 strands (1/2 pc)	50 strands (1 1/4 pc)
Size 2	10 strands (1/2 pc)	40 strands (1 pc)
Size 4	10 strands (1/2 pc)	40 strands (1 pc)

Loop the indicated piece of Sili Legs around the thread to obtain the correct number of strands.

Fly Dimensions -

	Size 2/0	Size 1/0	Size 1	Size 2	Size 4
Eye to back of head	3/8"	3/8"	5/16"	5/16"	1/4"
Eye to end of skirt	2 1/4"	2 1/8"	2"	1 3/4"	1 1/2"
Eye to end of tail	3"	2 7/8"	2 3/4"	2 1/4"	1 7/8"

Harness Dimensions -

	Size 2/0	Size 1/0	Size 1	Size 2	Size 4
Eye to hook*	1 1/8"	1 1/16"	1"	1"	15/16"
Eye to swivel	9/16"	1/2"	1/2"	1/2"	7/16"

*The loop for the hook eye should be approximately 1/4" long. The 1/4" loop in included in the measurements above

Blade Sizes -

Size 2/0	#4
Size 1/0	#3
Size 1	#2
Size 2	#2
Size 4	#1

Spinner Bait (Lumaflex)

Another interesting skirting material is Lumaflex. Lumaflex is a spandex material, it has a nice satiny sheen to it, and it has a lot of action in the water. It also has the advantage of being very light.

Lumaflex is sold in pre-made, banded, spinner bait skirts, but I have never found any of the pre-made skirts of designed for the heave-and-crank crowd to be useful for fly tying. That leaves us with spools. Unfortunately, spools are unhandy for tying, so you will need to prepare bundles of Lumaflex strands before you start tying.

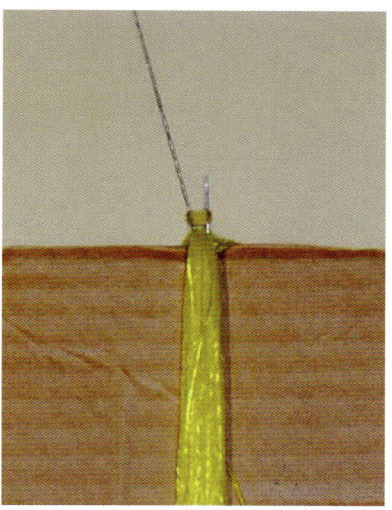

Start out by cutting a piece of cardboard about three or four inches wide. I make these bundles in two sizes, for the smaller flies (number 4 hook size) I use a piece of cardboard four inches long, and for the other size flies, I use a piece of cardboard six inches long. Wind the lumaflex around the cardboard, taking care not to apply any stretch to the material. A very slight stretch, magnified enough times will cause your cardboard to look like a taco shell. After you have loosely wrapped about a 1/2" or maybe about a pencil's thickness on each side of the cardboard, slide a stout piece of wire under the wraps on one end of the bundle. I use a spinner wire, they type used for building Mepps style in-line spinners for spin-fishermen. Once you have the wire looped under the bundle of Lumaflex strands, slide a small rubber band, made from a piece of 1/4" surgical tubing over the two ends of the wire to help hold the Lumaflex strands in place. With the wire and the rubber band in place, carefully slide the cardboard out of the bundle. Take care to keep the bundle together in the loop of wire. After you have the bundle free, roll the rubber band up onto the bundle of Lumaflex, so that it is holding the bundle tightly. Use your scissors to cut the loops left at the opposite end of the rubber band, and you are ready to tie. Keep in mind, this set-up is not as tough as a bundle of Krystal Flash. The rubber band can slip if you don't use care. If you can find good plastic tie-downs, they will work as well, perhaps even better. Of course, you might have to pay more for them.

Place the hook low in the vise, so that the jaws of the vise grip the hook just slightly down the bend of the hook. This will help us later when we are stretching the skirting material during the tying process. If the hook is gripped by the vise too far down the bend of the hook, there is a greater tendency for the hook to slip in the vise, or for the hook to bend when rearward pressure is exerted on the hook in the tying process.

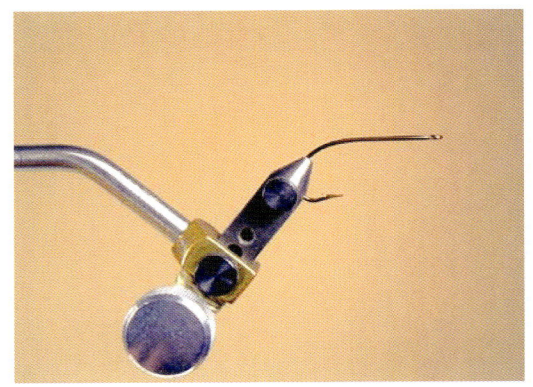

Start the thread on the hook and wind it back to just above the hook point. This is where we will begin tying in the tail. The body will actually start farther back on the hook shank, but we will need room between the tail tie-in point and the back of the body.

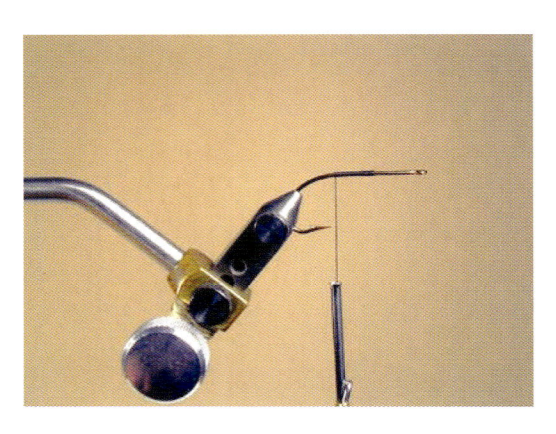

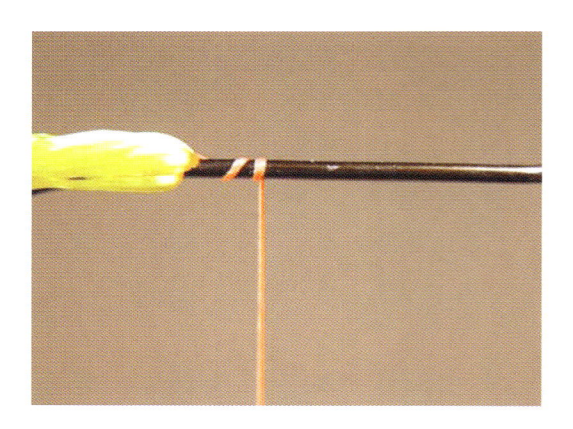

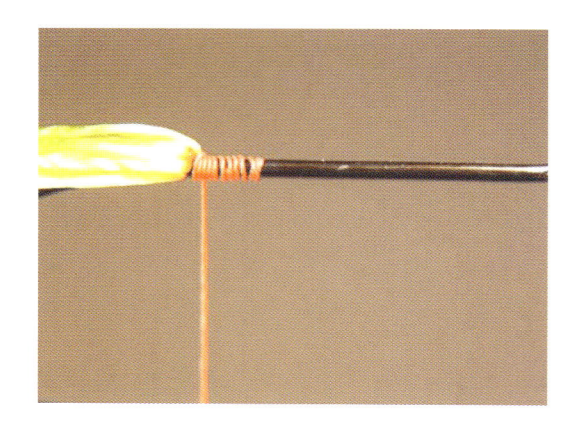

Count out one half the amount of strands of Lumaflex called for in the pattern chart for the size fly you are tying, and carefully, cut them off of your bundle. (Using half the amount called for will result in the correct amount when they are doubled.) Loop these pieces of Lumaflex around the thread. Holding the ends of the Lumaflex strands in your left hand, bring the thread up and over the hook shank and secure them to the top of the hook. When bringing the thread on around the hook, make a wide loop forward, rather than coming straight down on the other side of the hook. At the end of this wide forward wrap, make one more wrap of thread around the hook shank. The thread should now be approximately 1/8" to 1/4" in front, or toward the eye, from the tail tie-in point. Wind the tread tightly back to the tail tie-in point. This wide loop forward and the tight wraps back over it will help secure the tail strands to the tie-in point.

Stretch the tail strands to the rear. Stretching the Lumaflex reduces its diameter, and reduces the bulk caused by the tail, allowing us to make a smoother body. After you have stretched the tail sufficiently far, wind the thread tightly back over the tail to the end of the hook shank. Make a couple of secure wraps with the tying thread to hold it in that position, wind the thread back to the tie in point, and release the pressure on the tail.

Lumaflex is lighter than other skirting materials I commonly use, so the choice of body materials is not critical. However, since it is lighter, I go ahead and take advantage of this fact, and use a chenille for the body that is light-weight, and will not accumulate much water. (I often take advantage of this lighter weight and use a size larger spinner blade.) Estaz or Cactus chenille is made of Mylar, so it is lighter than regular chenille, and will not absorb water, so it seems like the best choice. We can also take advantage of the many interesting colors, including opalescent and dyed opalescent colors in these materials to end up with some interesting color effects.

Tie the Estaz in at the tail, and wind the thread forward to the correct point, indicated on the pattern chart, for the back of the head. Be sure to leave the appropriate space for the head. Failure to leave enough head space on this, or any of the spinner-bait flies will result in an unpleasant tying experience, and, usually, an unattractive fly. While winding the Estaz forward, keep pulling the fibers back out of the way with your left hand, so that none of the fibers are tied down by successive wraps. The long fibers on the Estaz will help with the appearance of bulk in the fly. When you get to the front of the body, tie and cut off the Estaz.

Wind the thread forward, and stop approximately one hook-eye width behind the hook-eye. Count out 1/4 of the strands called for on the pattern chart for the fly you are tying. (When these are looped around the thread and tied in, it will be 1/2 of the skirt. Loop these strands around the tying thread, and hold them with your left hand. While holding the ends in your left hand, bring the tying thread up and around the hook shank, and secure it on the far side. The thread wrap that binds the Lumaflex strands to the hook needs to be another wide loop forward that stops right behind the hook eye. Wind the tying thread tightly back to the tie-in point. Again, this wide loop, tied down tightly with the thread will enable us to stretch the skirt strands without any slippage.

Stretch the skirt strands to the rear of the hook as far as possible without breaking any. Lumaflex is very tough, and I have never had any problem with it breaking during the tying process. Wind the tying thread tightly over the Lumaflex strands back to the tie in point for the body. Make a few secure wraps, and wind the thread back to approximately one hook-eye length behind the hook-eye as before. Repeat the process on the near side of the hook. Again, 1/4 of the strands needed will, when doubled around the thread, form the other half of the skirt. Make the wide loop forward, and the tight wraps back to the tie-in point. Stretch the skirt strands back and wind the thread tightly back to the body of the fly.

Make a few secure wraps with the tying thread to anchor everything in place and wind the thread back to the tie in point.

At this point, we need to make sure that the skirt appears uniform all the way around the hook. Grab some of the strands of the skirt on the top of the fly, and gently stretch them upward, making a gently back and forth rocking motion to help even up the skirt. Do the same thing on the bottom of the fly. Rotate the fly to see that the skirt appears to completely encircle the fly.

Now it is time to cover up the butt ends of the skirt with the thread and build it up into a neat bullet shape. Keep in mind that the head needs to be large enough to enable us to paint eyes on each side. It can be difficult to make the head of the fly completely smooth and even using the rod wrapping thread. The thread is round, and will not flatten out as you are tying. If you are concerned that this will not look smooth and slick enough, you can tie off the rod wrapping thread at any point after the skirt has been tied down, and finish building the head with some flat waxed nylon thread.

I usually just use the rod wrapping thread, and do the best I can in making the head appear smooth. I know I am going to coat the head with at least two coats of cement, plus I am going to paint eyes on it, so a lot of the imperfections left on the head, caused by the Lumaflex, will not be noticeable. The important thing is to try and eliminate as many bumps and bulges, caused by the butt ends of the Lumaflex, as possible.

After you have the head wound to the shape you want, whip finish and cut off the thread.

At this point it is time to cut the skirt to length. Check the dimensions needed for the eye to the end of skirt for the size fly you are tying, and measure that distance from the eye of the hook to the

41

end of some of the skirt strands on top of the hook. Hold on to the skirt that covers the top of the fly with your left hand and, without stretching the skirt any, make the cut. Now that the skirt on the top of the fly is the correct length, fold all of the skirt strands forward and, using the strands that you just cut for a guide, cut the rest of the strands off evenly.

Check the dimensions needed for the eye of the hook to the end of the tail for the size of fly you are tying. Hold the strands of the tail with your left hand and, again, without stretching them, measure the correct distance and cut the tail to length.

If any additional adjustments are needed to make the skirt appear evenly distributed around the hook shank, you can make small adjustments, again, by stretching the skirt strands and gently rocking them back and forth.

It is now time to take the fly out of the vise and apply first coat of head cement. This coat of cement will protect the thread head and ensure it does not unravel. It will also provide a hard and solid base for painting the eyes on. Coat the head with enough cement to cover the threads as thoroughly as possible, without leaving enough to run and drip down onto the skirt. Hang the fly up by the eye until it has thoroughly dried.

After the head cement has dried, it is time to paint the eyes. I find the best way to apply the paint is to shake up the bottle of paint, take off the cap, and use the residual paint in the cap to for dipping your eye dowel. Select an eye dowel with a tip approximately the same size as the diameter of the head of the fly—or perhaps just a little smaller. Dip the dowel in the paint just enough to wet the tip, and touch it to each side of the head. The eye will most likely not appear round since the head of the fly curves away from the flat surface of the dowel. This can be corrected by touching the eye several times in a circular area. The overall appearance will be a circle. I have found that a slight oval shape to the eye looks even better than a small round eye. A prominent eye vastly adds to the overall appearance of the fly. After the first color is applied, hang the fly up once again, and allow it to dry.

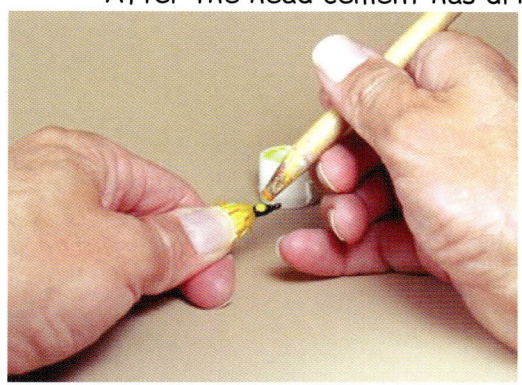

Next, select a smaller dowel, and the next color for the eye, and repeat the painting process. I usually paint the eye with each additional color moved to the front of the previous one, to give the overall appearance of the fly "looking" forward. An interesting effect can also be attained by placing each subsequent layer toward the back of the previous layer, giving the effect that the fly is "looking" back at something that might be chasing it. Use your imagination—the fish like them all. When you are done, return the fly to the drying rack.

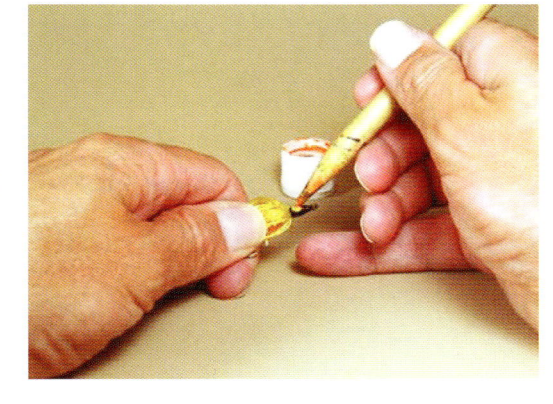

The last step in painting the eye is to paint a small black pupil. Again, this can be centered, in the front, back, or anywhere you like the effect. And again, hang the fly up to dry.

After the eyes have dried thoroughly, it is time for another coat of head cement. This coat will give the head a finished, glossy look, and will protect the eye and the threads. In the event that you choose to use Hard-As-Nails for the cement, care must be taken to keep the cement from dissolving the eyes and causing them to smear out. In this case, allow plenty of time for the eyes to completely dry—a couple of days if you can. When you put the cement over the eyes, make no more brush strokes than are absolutely necessary. Usually, you have time for one or two quick strokes over the eye before the paint softens enough to be affected by the brush. A third or fourth brush stroke may be one too many. Water based cements do not have this problem, and you will have more time to apply the coat. Put the cement on evenly, and, once again, return the fly to it's place on the drying rack.

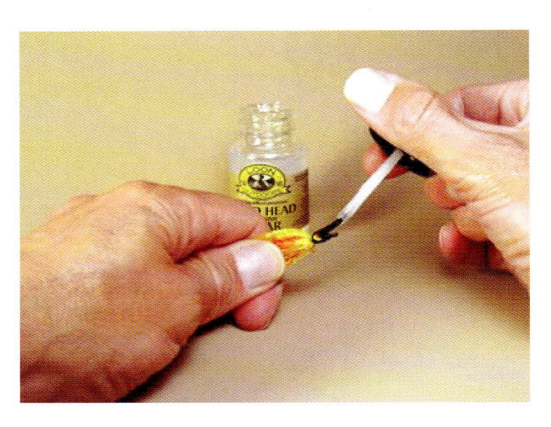

When the fly is dry, it is time to build the wire harness.

44

Spinner Bait (Lumaflex)

Hook: Mustad 3366 sizes 2/0 - 4
Thread: Size A rod wrapping thread
Tail: Lumaflex
Body: Estaz
Skirt: Lumaflex
Head: Thread built up in a bullet shape, one coat of cement under, and one coat over the eyes
Eyes: Acrylic paint; black over fluorescent orange over fluorescent yellow on black thread; black over fluorescent yellow over fluorescent red on white thread
Wire: .022" trolling wire
Swivel: Size 10 barrel swivel
Split Rings: Size 10
Spinner: Indiana

Colors -

	Tail	Body	Skirt	Thread
Black	Black	Black (#21)	Black	Black
White	White	Fl. Yellow (#24)	White	White
Chartreuse	Chartreuse	Pearl (#02)	Chartreuse	White
Yellow	Yellow	Pearl orange (#31)	Yellow	Black
Fuchsia	Fuchsia	Pearl orange (#31)	Fuchsia	Black

Skirt and Tail -

	Tail	Skirt
Size 2/0	20 strands	56 strands
Size 1/0	18 strands	52 strands
Size 1	16 strands	48 strands
Size 2	12 strands	44 strands
Size 4	10 strands	40 strands

For the tail, loop 1/2 the indicated number of strands of Lumaflex around the thread; for the skirt, loop 1/4 the

Fly Dimensions -

	Size 2/0	Size 1/0	Size 1	Size 2	Size 4
Eye to back of head	3/8"	3/8"	5/16"	5/16"	1/4"
Eye to end of skirt	2 1/4"	2 1/8"	2"	1 3/4"	1 1/2"
Eye to end of tail	3"	2 7/8"	2 3/4"	2 1/4"	1 7/8"

Harness Dimensions -

	Size 2/0	Size 1/0	Size 1	Size 2	Size 4
Eye to hook*	1 1/8"	1 1/16"	1"	1"	15/16"
Eye to swivel	9/16"	1/2"	1/2"	1/2"	7/16"

*The loop for the hook eye should be approximately 1/4" long. The 1/4" loop in included in the measurements above

Blade Sizes -

Size 2/0 #4
Size 1/0 #3
Size 1 #2
Size 2 #2
Size 4 #1

Others

And I hope you don't feel the need to stop there. Other materials can be used as well. There is Flashabou, Krystal Flash, marabou, and any number of synthetic or natural hairs that can be used for some variation. One good alternative is the feather duster spinner bait. The feather duster is made out of hackle, usually the large or webby stuff that isn't any good for smaller flies. Tie on a hackle tail with the hackle flared out, and then wind a good thick hackle body. Imagination is the key.

Feather Duster Spinner Bait

Casting and Fishing the Fly Rod Spinner Bait

I will not try to include all the techniques and intricacies of casting and fishing the fly rod spinner bait—mainly because I am sure I don't know them all. I might try to relate a few of these techniques to help you get started, but then it's up to you. In fact, I would appreciate any new ideas you can come up with.

Casting – Regardless of how light we might try to make a fly rod spinner bait, it still comes out being heavier than, say, a #14 light Cahill. Accordingly, we might need to adjust our casting methods just a little. Keep in mind that the real definition of fly fishing (according to me) is fishing an artificial lure where the weight of the line is used to propel the lure to its intended destination. As long as the weight of the line is heavier than the weight of the lure (fly) you are fly fishing. Fly rod spinner baits weigh in with the heavier, but not the heaviest, of the available flies. Many of the larger weighted trout nymphs actually weigh more, especially when you factor in the weight of the split-shot commonly used in nymph fishing.

A size 2/0 fly rod spinner bait averages about 1/8 ounce in weight—pretty heavy for a fly. But when we balance this with the weight of the first 30 feet of a 9 weight fly line, which is just over 1/2 ounce, we see the fly line weighing over 4 times as much as the fly, which is certainly enough to control the fly. Similarly on the other end of the spectrum, a size 4 fly rod spinner bait averages a little less than 1/16 ounce. The first 30 feet of a 5 weight fly line weighs in at around 1/3 ounce—over 5 times as much as the fly. I don't know the actual fly line-to-fly weight ratio that will cause the fly casting process to completely break down, but the ratios listed above seem to perform suitably well. A name like Mel Kreiger on your name tag might make a difference here.

The real consideration in casting a fly rod spinner bait is the spinner blade. When you start to pick the fly up to make a cast, the spinner blade goes wild. The resistance of the blade is no different than weight to the rod. When you begin your back cast, the rod quickly becomes overloaded. When the spinner breaks free of the water, the rod suddenly isn't overloaded any more. However, it is bent more than would normally be expected for the amount of weight it is attempting to cast, and will rapidly straighten out. The rod will, in effect, try to make the back cast faster than the fly and fly line is ready to go. A little compensation in the timing of your back cast will be necessary in order to load the rod properly for the forward cast. In order to reduce the "weight" of the spinner before it leaves the water, make sure the fly is close to the surface before picking it up for the next cast. If it has sunk down very deep, make a roll cast to get the fly closer to the surface before making your back-cast.

I find I like a slower action rod when casting spinner baits. In fact, a good ol' fiberglass rod is just about right, though one of the slower action graphite will do as well.
Fast action rods will work, but the timing is even more critical. The rod may have finished its part of the back-cast before the line and the fly catch up with it. As with anything else in this sport, nothing will guarantee success like practice.

Fishing – The best advice I can give on fishing the fly rod spinner bait is try everything. Try everything until something works. Slow retrieves, quick strips. Fish it close to the surface, let it sink a while. It all works, sometimes.

The fly rod spinner bait really comes into its own in off-colored water. When the fish are feeding sub-surface, but can't see any distance in the water, they can hear the spinner blade. At these times it helps to keep the fly moving in the water. When the blade stops, the fish can't find it, and you may miss a strike. A fast hand-twist retrieve will usually keep the spinner blade spinning, and keep the fly moving slowly through the water.

Fly rod spinner baits will run with the blade down, as the blade is the heaviest part of the fly. While it is not completely weedless, the blade will help it ride over logs or rocks in the water, making it somewhat weedless. Of course, if you stop your retrieve, the weedless quality of the spinning spinner blade diminishes rapidly. You will notice, if you make a long strip, that the torque of the blade will slowly cause the fly to rotate as it moves forward. As soon as the forward motion stops, the fly will return to its blade-down position.

As I mentioned earlier, sharp hooks are important. On most strikes, the fly is moving, and you will have no doubt when to set the hook. In fact, most of the time the fish hooks itself without you really having to do anything but pull it in. However, if the fish grabs it in between strips, you won't necessarily feel it. It is those times that the sharp hook really pays off. At times, allowing the fly to sink on its own will cause the blade to spin slowly, and will induce a strike.

I have caught most types of warm-water fish on spinner baits, and I am quite sure the ones I haven't caught are not the fault of the fish. I feel pretty confident that if you put a fly rod spinner bait in front of the right fish at the right time, you will catch it. You might even be able to catch a trout on one, though I don't know why you would want to let a trout slobber all over a perfectly good bass fly.

Use an 8 or 9 weight rod when you are fishing the larger sized spinner baits, and a 5 or 6 on the smaller ones. Again, it is a matter of the line you are casting weighing more than the fly you are casting. Accordingly, don't try to cast much under 20 or 30 feet. And again, if your drivers license doesn't say Mel Kreiger, don't try any 100 foot casts. Catch the closer ones, and then paddle or walk over closer to the ones you couldn't reach before.

Fly fishing with fly rod spinner baits is what traditional fly fishing would look like if Isaac Walton had lived in Lake Charles, Louisiana.

Sources

Most of the materials use to tie fly rod spinner baits can be purchased at any of the usual fly shops in your area, or any of the mail-order shops you normally send your money to. Some of the more difficult materials (at least for fly tyers) can be found at many of the following retailers:

Cabela's
1 Cabela Drive
Sidney, NE 69160
800-237-4444
fax: 800-496-6329
web site: www.cabelas.com

Bass Pro Shops
2500 E. Kearney
Springfield, MO 65898-0123
800-227-7776
fax: 800-566-4600
web site: www.basspro.com

Bob Marriott's Flyfishing Store
2700 W. Orangethorpe Avenue
Fullerton, CA 92833
800-535-6633
fax: 800-367-2299
info@bobmarriotts.com
web site: bobmarriotts.com

Living Rubber Company
P.O. Box 245
Merlin, OR 97532
(541) 471-1248
fax: (541) 471-1249
livingrubber@livingrubber.net
web site: http://livingrubber.com/

Lurecraft
7129 E 46th Street
Indianapolis, IN 46226-3803
800-925-9088
fax: 317-549-3893
lurecraft@iquest.net
web site: www.lurecraft.com

Jann's Netcraft
P.O. Box 89
Maumee, OH 43537-0089
800-638-2723
fax: 419-868-8338
web site: www.jannsnetcraft.com

Tackle-Craft
P.O. Box 280
Chippewa Falls, WI 54729-0280
715-723-3645
fax: 715-723-2489
tacklecr@aol.com

Barlow's Tackle Shop
Box 830369
Richardson, TX 75083
1-800-707-0208
web site: www.barlowstackle.com

LEARN MORE ABOUT FISHING WITH THESE BOOKS

TYING EMERGERS
Jim Schollmeyer and Ted Leeson

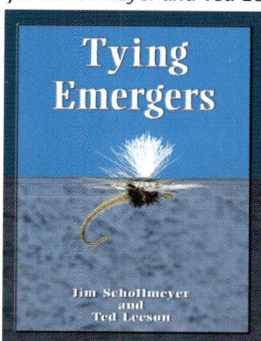

Two of fly-fishing's most well-respected writers collaborate once again, this time discussing emergers. Emergence is itself a behavior, and it puts the tier in a challenging and rather unusual position—not that of imitating a fixed and recognizable form of the insect, but rather of representing a process. This book shows you how, including: emerger design and materials, basic tying techniques, many specialized tying techniques, fly patterns, and more. When you buy a book by these two authors you know what you will get—up-to-the-minute information, well-written text, and superb photography, Tying Emergers will not let you down. 8 1/2 x 11 inches, 344 pages.

SB: $45.00 ISBN: 1-57188-306-1
UPC: 0-81127-00140-8

Spiral HB: $60.00 ISBN: 1-57188-307-X
UPC: 0-81127-00141-5

FEDERATION OF FLY FISHERS FLY PATTERN ENCYCLOPEDIA
Over 1600 of the Best Fly Patterns
Edited by Al & Gretchen Beatty

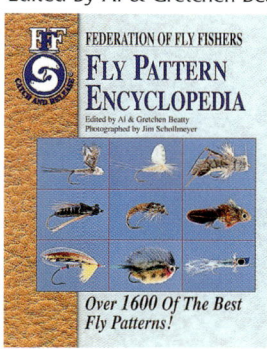

Simply stated, this book is a Federation of Fly Fishers' conclave taken to the next level, a level that allows the reader to enjoy the learning and sharing in the comfort of their own home. The flies, ideas, and techniques shared herein are from the "best of the best" demonstration fly tiers North America has to offer. The tiers are the famous as well as the unknown with one simple characteristic in common; they freely share their knowledge.

As you leaf through these pages, you will get from them just what you would if you spent time in the fly tying area at any FFF function. At such a show, if you dedicate time to observing the individual tiers, you can learn the information, tips, or tricks they are demonstrating. Full color, 8 1/2 x 11 inches, 232 pages.

SB: $39.95 ISBN: 1-57188-208-1
UPC: 0-66066-00422-2

ROD CRAFTING
Jeffrey L. Hatton

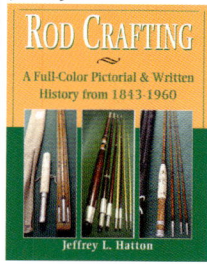

This unique, one-of-a-kind book is a must for anyone interested in the history of our great sport and collectors of antique fishing tackle. It takes a look at the history of fishing rods from the early 1800s to the 1970s, through text and hundreds of color photographs. With access to five private and extensive collections, Hatton covers the first three ages of rod-making: The smith age, up to 1870; the expansion era, 1870-1900; and the classic era, 1900-1970s. Forty-nine beautiful rods are featured, each with a description, history, notable features, and much more. Be warned: once you get into this book, you may look up to discover that several hours have gone by.

SB: $45.00 ISBN: 1-57188-356-8
UPC: 0-81127-00190-3

HB: $65.00 ISBN: 1-57188-357-6
UPC: 0-81127-00191-0

MAYFLIES: TOP TO BOTTOM
Shane Stalcup

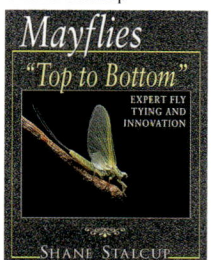

Shane Stalcup approaches fly-tying with the heart and mind of both a scientist and an artist. His realistic approach to imitating the mayfly is very popular and effective across the West, and can be applied to waters across North America. Mayflies are the most important insects to trout fishermen, and in this book, Shane shares his secrets for tying effective, life-like mayfly imitations that will bring fly-anglers more trout. Many tying techniques and materials are discussed, Mayflies: Top to Bottom is useful to beginner and expert tiers alike. 8 1/2 x 11 inches, 157 pages.

SB: $29.95 ISBN: 1-57188-242-1
UPC: 0-66066-00496-3

Spiral HB: $39.95 ISBN: 1-57188-243-X
UPC: 0-81127-00116-3

CURTIS CREEK MANIFESTO
Sheridan Anderson

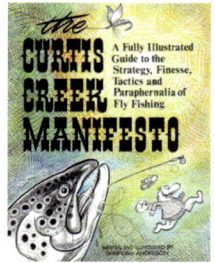

Finest beginner fly-fishing guide due to its simple, straightforward approach. It is laced with outstanding humor provided in its hundreds of illustrations. All the practical information you need to know is presented in an extremely delightful way such as rod, reel, fly line and fly selection, casting, reading water, insect knowledge to determine which fly pattern to use, striking and playing fish, leaders and knot tying, fly tying, rod repairs, and many helpful tips. A great, easy-to-understand book. 8 1/2 x 11 inches, 48 pages.

SB: $7.95 ISBN: 0-936608-06-4
UPC: 0-81127-00113-2

WESTERN MAYFLY HATCHES
Rick Hafele & Dave Hughes

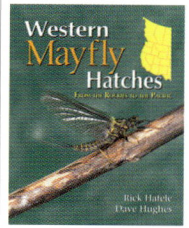

Western Mayfly Hatches introduces the mayflies important in the western states and provinces, shows how to recognize them, helps in the selection of fly patterns to match them, and provides the best presentation methods. Also included is: matching hatches, collecting and observing mayflies, recognizing species and stages, fly-tying techniques, and more. For each species there's a detailed illustration labeled with the characteristics of each life stage, and individual charts of emergence times and hatch importance provide even more information. *Western Mayfly Hatches* leaves no stone unturned. 8 1/2 x 11 inches, 268 pages.

SB: $39.95 ISBN: 1-57188-304-5
UPC: 0-81127-00138-5

HB: $60.00 ISBN: 1-57188-305-3
UPC: 0-81127-00139-2

Limited HB: $125.00 ISBN: 1-57188-337-1
UPC: 0-81127-00171-2

FLY TYING MADE CLEAR AND SIMPLE
Skip Morris

With over 220 color photographs, expert tier show all the techniques you need to know. 73 different materials and 27 tools. Clear, precise advice tells you how to do it step-by-step. Dries, wets, streamers, nymphs, etc., included so that you can tie virtually any pattern. 8 1/2 x 11 inches, 80 pages.

SPIRAL SB: $19.95 ISBN: 1-878175-130
UPC: 0-66066-00103-0

SOFTBOUND: $19.95 ISBN: 1-57188-231-6
UPC: 0-81127-00131-6

SMALL-STREAM FLY FISHING
Jeff Morgan

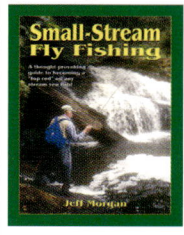

There are many myths surrounding small streams—they only hold small fish, they're for beginners and kids, they aren't a challenge, don't allow for versatility in techniques, and so on—in this book, Morgan addresses these myths and shares the realities of small-stream fishing. Topics covered include: the myths; best small-stream equipment; ecology; entomology and fly patterns; small-stream types; fly-fishing techniques; casting; reading the water; and more. If you're up for the challenge, maybe it's time to explore this fun and unique facet of fly-fishing. 8 1/2 x 11 inches, 142 pages.

SB: $24.95 ISBN: 1-57188-346-0
UPC: 0-81127-00180-4

**ASK FOR THESE BOOKS AT YOUR LOCAL TACKLE OR FLY SHOP.
IF UNAVAILABLE CALL, FAX, OR ORDER ON THE WEB AT WWW.AMATOBOOKS.COM**

Frank Amato Publications, Inc. • PO Box 82112 • Portland, Oregon 97282
TOLL FREE 1-800-541-9498 (8-5 Pacific Time) • FAX (503) 653-2766

LEARN MORE ABOUT FISHING WITH THESE BOOKS

THE FLY TIER'S BENCHSIDE REFERENCE TO TECHNIQUES AND DRESSING STYLES
Ted Leeson and Jim Schollmeyer

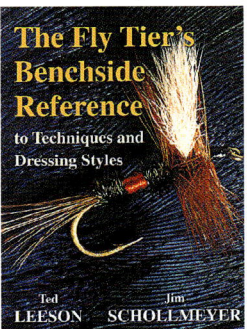

Printed in full color on top-quality paper, this book features over 3,000 color photographs and over 400,000 words describing and showing, step-by-step, hundreds of fly-tying techniques! Leeson and Schollmeyer have collaborated to produce this masterful volume which will be the standard fly-tying reference book for the entire trout-fishing world. Through enormous effort on their part they bring to all who love flies and fly fishing a wonderful compendium of fly-tying knowledge. Every fly tier should have this book in their library! All color, 8 1/2 by 11 inches, 464 pages, over 3,000 color photographs, index, hardbound with dust jacket.
HB: $100.00.   **ISBN: 1-57188-126-3**

DRY FLY FISHING
Dave Hughes

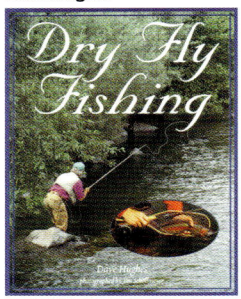

This beautifully written, all-color guide, will help make you a very competent dry-fly angler with chapters on: tackle, dry-fly selection, dry-fly casting techniques, fishing dry-flies on moving water and on lakes and ponds, hatches and matching patterns, and 60 of the best dries in color and with fly dressings. The information contained and attractive color presentation will really help you! 8 1/2 x 11 inches, 56 pages.
SB: $15.95   **ISBN: 1-878175-68-8**

HATCH GUIDE FOR NEW ENGLAND STREAMS
Thomas Ames, Jr.

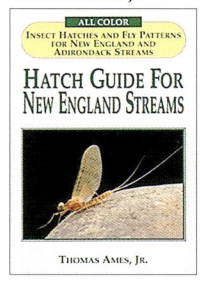

New England's streams, and the insects and fish that inhabit them, have their own unique qualities. Their flowing waters support an amazing diversity of insect species from all of the major orders.
   Hatch Guide to New England Streams, explores the insects of New England. Ames covers: reading water; presentations for New England streams; tackle; night fishing; and more. The bulk of this book, however, deals with the insects and the best flies to imitate them. Similar in style to Jim Schollmeyer's successful "Hatch Guide" series, Ames discusses the natural and its behaviors on the left-hand page and the three best flies to imitate it on the right. Tom's color photography of the naturals and their imitations is superb. A must for all New England fly-fishers! Full color. 4 1/8 x 6 1/8 inches, 272 pages; insect and fly plates.
SB: $19.95   **ISBN: 1-57188-210-3**

THE BENCHSIDE INTRODUCTION TO FLY TYING
Ted Leeson & Jim Schollmeyer

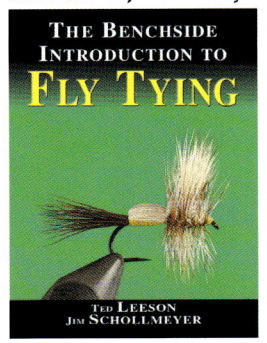

Renowned writing team Ted Leeson and Jim Schollmeyer have set another milestone in the world of fly tying with this unique new addition to their Benchside Reference series. Following the incredible success of *The Fly Tier's Benchside Reference*, Jim & Ted now offer the first beginner's book of fly tying to allow readers simultaneous access to fly recipes, tying steps, and techniques. No more flipping back and forth from fly pattern to technique, hoping the wings don't fall off your mayfly. The first 50 pages of this oversized, spiral-bound book are filled with impeccably photographed fly-tying techniques. The next 150 pages are cut horizontally across the page. The top pages show tying steps for dozens of fly patterns, including references to tying techniques that are explained step by step in the bottom pages. This groundbreaking book is sure to thrill all fly tiers. Over 1500 beautiful color photographs, 9 X 12 inches, 192 all-color pages.
SPIRAL HB: $45.00   **ISBN: 1-57188-369-X**

NYMPH FISHING
Dave Hughes

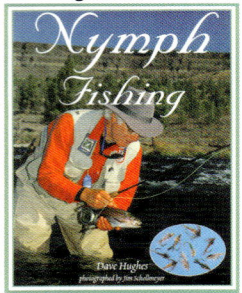

This masterful all-color, large format book by one of America's favorite angling writers will teach you what you need to know to fish nymphs effectively, with crisp text and dramatic color photos by Jim Schollmeyer. Color plates and dressings of author's favorite nymphs. All the techniques and methods learned here will guarantee that on the stream or lake your nymph imitation will be fishing right! 8 1/2 x 11 inches, 56 pages.
SB: $19.95   **ISBN: 1-57188-002-X**

HATCH GUIDE FOR LAKES
Naturals and Their Imitations for Stillwater Trout Fishing
Jim Schollmeyer

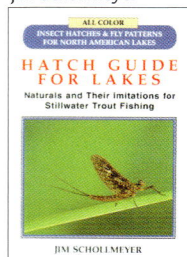

This "little lake Bible" organizes and explains lake types, how to read and fly fish them, and understand and imitate their aquatic insect life cycles—and nearby terrestrial insects. Next to each color insect photograph is a representative fly pattern. By carefully inspecting the lake for insects you can find the correct fly to use as shown in the book. *Hatch Guide for Lakes* is the golden key to unravelling one of fly fishing's last best-kept secrets. 4 x 5 inches, 162 pages.
SB: $15.00   **ISBN: 1-57188-324-X**

MATCHING MAYFLIES Everything You Need to Know to Match Any Mayfly You'll Ever Encounter
Dave Hughes

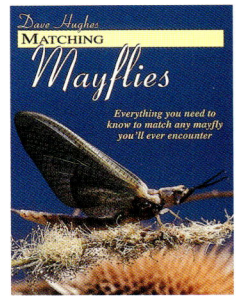

Mayflies are the most important order of aquatic insects to those who fly fish for trout. In order to fish their hatches successfully, it is essential to understand their four important stages—nymphs, emergers, duns, and spinners—and to carry and know when to use the best fly patterns for each phase of this life cycle.
   Dave has been studying mayfly hatches, photographing them, tying flies to match them, and honing presentation techniques to fish those flies for more than 30 years. Now you can benefit from Dave's vast on-stream knowledge. Full-color, 8 1/2 x 11 inches, 84 pages.
SB: $25.00   **ISBN: 1-57188-260-X**
SPIRAL HB: $39.95   **ISBN: 1-57188-261-8**

HOW FISH WORK
Dr. Tom Sholseth

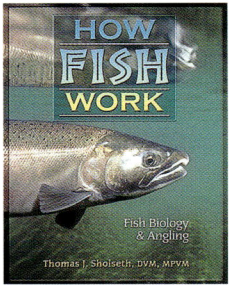

Anglers are scientists. In their own way, they observe and experiment with systematic methods of capturing their species of interest. There are lots of scientific principles used in angling—and, here, Tom Sholseth shares them in an entertaining and easy-to-follow way which is sure to increase the success of all fishermen. Sholseth discusses: what is "scientific angling"?; angler characteristics; the aquatic environment in which they fish; equipment; effect of different kinds of light on fish; their senses and behaviors; the predator/prey relationship; strike responses; handling fish; creating a field guide; how the placement of your lure or fly looks to the fish; how to design more effective fly patterns; everything you need to understand and appreciate the species for which you fish. 8 1/2 x 11 inches, 80 pages.
SB: $19.95   **ISBN: 1-57188-239-1**

HATCH GUIDE FOR WESTERN STREAMS
Jim Schollmeyer

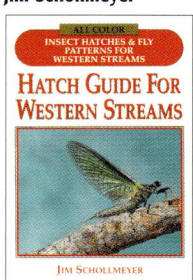

Successful fishing on Western streams requires preparation—you need to know what insects are emerging, when and where, and which patterns best match them. Now, thanks to Jim Schollmeyer, the guessing is over.
   Hatch Guide for Western Streams is the third in Jim's successful "Hatch Guide" series. Jim covers all you need for a productive trip on Western streams: water types you'll encounter; successful fishing techniques; identifying the major hatches, providing basic background information about these insects. Information is presented in a simple, clear manner. A full-color photograph of the natural is shown on the left-hand page, complete with its characteristics, habits and habitat; the right-hand page shows three flies to match the natural, including effective fishing techniques. 4 x 5 inches; full-color; 196 pages; fantastic photographs of naturals and flies.
SB: $19.95   **ISBN: 1-57188-109-3**

ASK FOR THESE BOOKS AT YOUR LOCAL TACKLE OR FLY SHOP.
IF UNAVAILABLE CALL, FAX, OR ORDER ON THE WEB AT WWW.AMATOBOOKS.COM

Frank Amato Publications, Inc. • PO Box 82112 • Portland, Oregon 97282
TOLL FREE 1-800-541-9498 (8-5 Pacific Time) • FAX (503) 653-2766